BEYOND MANAGEMENT

TOWARDS ESTABLISHING ETHICAL BUSINESS

ETSKO SCHUITEMA

Intent Publishing

COPYRIGHT

About our logo: The square in the middle represents The One, from The One come the two surrounding lines, the 'Outward' and the 'Inward'.

The next four are the 'Sensory' and 'Meaning' aspects of the 'Inward' and 'Outward', and the last eight, the 'Celestial' and 'Terrestrial' manifestations of the previous aspects.

CONTENTS

FOREWORD

Watching Etsko Schuitema grow into the authentic individual he has become has been an amazing process. I first met him as a younger colleague in the South Africa Mining Industry in 1984 and it is my pleasure to make the observation that this man has gone far beyond what the late Abraham Maslow called 'self-actualisation'. He has not only grown as a human being, but has also developed his remarkable talent for interacting with people. He knows exactly how and why leadership can empower people to become leaders themselves.

The insights which he so ably articulates in this book are fresh, basic and consistently helpful to all those who reflect on what they can do for others. The theme of generosity is addressed and captured clearly and sets a standard for the explanation, in essential terms, of the practical meaning of making a living in modern society. The potential impact of the book's authentic message on the sphere of management and much of organisational life is significant. He makes a fresh contribution to the role of benevolence in organisational systems, and introduces original perspectives in how to shift from mediocrity to virtuosity in the workplace. These will ensure healthy bottom-line earnings.

The concluding chapters successfully clarify the key issue of authenticity. In the increasingly globally-connected world in which we live, such an approach sets an inspiring example of how to deal with the tasks every manager faces.

This book, now reprinted for the third time, is valuable also for its thematic account of human communication which focuses on the core issue of credibility. The author has earned such credibility and his contribution deserves to reach the public. It exemplifies basic ethical guidance, especially to those who have been placed in a position of authority over others. Coping with such responsibility in the workplace is the subject of this book.

Readers in this position will be challenged to recognise themselves as individual and discover the characteristic of authenticity within themselves which will in turn inspire the effective development of the people who report to them.

Volker Hooyberg
Department of Communication Science, University of Zululand

Seldom have I been so honoured and excited by something as the author's request that I write the foreword of this work. There is undeniably a touch of nepotism in my views, but I cannot adequately express the fundamental impact that exposure to the author's insights over the past number of years has had on my professional life.

Thirty years of intimate contact with the economic environment as a professional financial journalist and broadcaster formed a basis of understanding that I believed was whole and complete. But this cannot compare with the insights Etsko and his work have given me in the last few years.

In this book you will find a key that goes far beyond understanding the true dynamics of business, organisational and economic structures. It goes beyond the cutting edge of any of the most advanced management theory, incisively and surgically removing the management school hocus pocus that has muddled our economic lives to nearly beyond salvation.

The most profound statement of all – that we are on this earth to give not get – is at the same time unpalatable and the most challenging. At first, I too responded to these conclusions with the jaundiced journalist's eye. Until the overwhelming implications of this truly old world logic started to dawn and influence my very being.

For that I am deeply indebted to the author. If, upon reading this book, you experience only a fraction of what I have, your life would have changed forever.

Jerry Schuitema

Chapter 1

INTRODUCTION

There is a current euphoria reflected in the media regarding the New World Order and the New South Africa. Utopia, it seems, is just around the corner with a promise of liberal democracy and freedom for all. From one point of view this rash of fevered Utopianism can only be viewed as theatre which no one but the very naïve actually believes.

The reason for this is that, economically speaking, the world is in a shambles. There are only a few examples where the great technocratic dream can be said to be a success, and in many instances its great stalwarts (such as America) are in such a state of decay that utter collapse is not just possible, but inevitable.

So, rather than being truly optimistic and contented, the person living in the shadow of this crumbling edifice is in a state of despair. In some cases, like South Africa, this discontent manages to express itself in an overt political and revolutionary manner, but in most instances people have just experienced too much of this kind of puppetry to expect it to have much to offer. Mostly, it is to be found in a general feeling of social malaise that expresses itself in things such as a generation of head-banging, promiscuous youth and, most importantly, in an unbridled acquisitiveness that has, for example, made the total debt of private persons in the United Kingdom greater than the national debt of Brazil.

From one point of view, personal debt may be viewed as a barometer of discontent because it is evidence of need. People are unhappy and in a state of want because of what they do not have, and cannot have by their own means. So they willingly place themselves in a weakened, indebted position in order to satisfy their want. The tragedy is, of course, that this is a vicious circle. The more one acquires in this way, the more at risk and weaker one becomes, falling ever deeper into that fearful hole of need. The truth is that technocratic man is vulnerable, weakened and in need, and desperately has to have in order to be fulfilled. But, the more he has, the worse his existential discomfort becomes.

Synonymous to being in need is the feeling of being small. Happiness is in the hands of the bank manager, your employer or some other dispenser of 'goodies'. It is up to them to make you well, and if you are not well, the fault lies with them. They have turned you into a victim and you are at their mercy. And so you accuse them, revile them, or even mobilize against them under the banner of the party if you are gullible because you honestly believe that their having and your not having is the result of their withholding from you that which is rightfully yours.

But, more than likely, you would be too tired for such juvenile antics, and you would confine yourself to fulfilling in the application forms for buying a video machine on credit. You still remain the needy supplicant, and the victim in the hands of some 'Big Brother' institution, while being perfectly aware that your weakness and dependence on it is in its interest, not yours.

"There is no such thing as a free lunch" you think to yourself as you reflect on the interest they are going to charge on the money you are borrowing to buy the video machine. You know that you want and have to get something, just as you know that by 'giving', Big Brother is in fact getting from you. Both of you want as much as possible for as little as possible, but what really troubles you is that the dice are loaded in his favour, which they must be because, after all, you are the supplicant.

To understand discontent, therefore, is to understand 'victimhood'. The victim is that resentful being sitting in organisations and society (and not necessarily at the bottom) feeling that those in charge are big, bad and horrible and primarily in the relationship to maximize their benefit from the victim. So the victim feels that it is perfectly legitimate to get away with as much as possible, to maximize his own benefit!

In the case of the 'tired' or 'mature' victim, his taking back will include anything from stealing the boss's time and his pencils to plain indolence. This attitude was dryly described by Piet Pretorius, an Underground Manager at West Driefontein. "We are living", in the age of the 'slops'!

The juvenile victim, also known as the angry young man, is the entertaining fool who helps to keep the media filled with sordid material for your consumption and edification. He is the robber of banks, the necklacer of neighbours and the saboteur of production facilities.

Essentially, however, both these victims are the same people. They are takers. The most disturbing fact about them is that they believe that their behaviour is perfectly legitimate: "Because you are big and bad, I (the victim) am good and all the things I do to get even are therefore not only acceptable, but just and praiseworthy. " And since so-called liberalism has taught us to support the underdog, we blithely accept this logic.

The result of all this is an intolerable state of affairs. In short it implies that people believe it is correct for them to give less and demand more. The consistent wail one hears about rights (worker rights, animal rights, human rights) is part of this illness. It amounts to the mentality that there are certain minimum conditions that have to be met by 'them' (the bosses, society) which are viewed as a baseline, irrespective of what the person protected by those rights is giving. Popular debate is entrenching more and more of these rights, giving rise to the situation that, on an international scale, there is an increase in expectations and a decrease in aspirations. People are expecting ever more but are only prepared to work for and give ever less.

This has obvious implications for productivity at the organisational level, and the creation of wealth, or the production of surpluses, in more general terms. The creation of a surplus implies that a group of people are working together to produce something that is bigger than the sum of the parts which individual participants are taking or receiving from the system. In other words, surpluses are created by people who give more than they take. Victims can thus not be party to the creation of surpluses because they feel it is legitimate for them to take more than they give.

Understanding and redressing victimhood and discontent are therefore the key issues of our time and it is to this debate that I wish to contribute with this book.

The aim of this work is to gain insight into the idea of victimhood and the issue of empowerment since victimhood may essentially be understood as a state of powerlessness.

The text is divided into three major sections which provide mutually conditioning statements on the matter at hand. Chapters 1 and 2 deal directly with the problem of discontent in the workplace, and the role of leadership in addressing the problem. It could therefore be regarded as an examination of the nature of the empowering relationship between the superordinate and subordinate at work.

The second section (chapters 3 and 4) deals with that which needs to be done to establish correct leadership, while the third section (chapters 5 and 6) deals with the empowered individual and his relationship with the world. The aim of this discussion is not necessarily existential. Rather, it focuses on the challenge of creating an authentic sense of empowered stewardship of the organisation and its aims among all its members.

Chapter 2

THE DISCONTENTED AT WORK

In 1982 I was employed by the Human Resources Laboratory of the Chamber of Mines Research Organisation to work on a project that had, as its focus, the problem of employee discontent. The job was a fascinating one, not just because the activity was research, but more so because of the industry served by the Research Organisation.

At the time the South African gold mining industry was a monstrously large affair employing half a million people, most of whom where black migrant workers from various rural areas throughout Southern Africa. The main labour supply areas were Transkei, Lesotho and Mozambique, roughly in that order in terms of number of men supplied.

Job reservation was still very much in force, which meant that blacks basically did the low-skilled and labour-intensive work, while most senior positions were reserved for whites. Black employees were mainly house in large, single sex hostels where they were accommodated in dormitories that had, on average, 16 men to a room. Family accommodation for black employees was reserved for a select group of clerical personnel. Most whites, on the other hand, lived with their families in houses, provided by the mines.

Because most of the mines involved in our study were deep-level operations (one even reaching 3.8km underground), the work was both dangerous and stressful. Routine problems that had to be con- tended with in the workplace included landslides, seismic events and poor ventilation, all of which could prove fatal.

In light of these conditions it was obvious that employee discontent would be an important issue for investigation by any group of behavioural scientists employed to serve the industry. Much of the research done was concerned with conflict, a phenomenon that had cost the industry vast amounts of money. Large-scale mobilizations of black employees were not uncommon in the industry. These were frequently riotous and resulted in injury, loss of life and damage to the mining facilities.

Much of the conflict research was carried out by Kent Macnamara, to whose project I was assigned on joining the laboratory. Macna- mara's approach to the study of conflict was primarily historical and involved the collection and analysis of recorded incidences of conflict in order to arrive at an understanding of the underlying trends. Clearly, although this work was of tremendous academic importance, it contained an element of shutting the stable door once the horse had bolted. One could say that it was not tremendously *useful* to the industry merely to find out that people had – once again – been killed. We had to find a way to identify *potentially* explosive situations, i.e. to uncover them before they occurred. It was to this end that I was instructed to develop an opinion survey instrument for assessing the climate of employee opinion on mines.

This survey instrument looked at a plethora of issues, including views of trust in management and supervision, unions, and views of physical conditions, conditions of service, management communications and problem-solving roles. However, it was clear that in order to make any sense of such a mass of data, one would have to focus on a single issue or a core of issues, which would then serve as an essential diagnostic measurement to which all other areas could be related. On examining the available literature we decided to take trust in management as the central diagnostic measurement, the argument being that if people trusted their managers they were basically happy, and if they distrusted them they were essentially discontented.

We used a quantitative method to assess trust, asking employees if they found management to be highly trustworthy, reasonable trustworthy, not very trustworthy or totally untrustworthy, or whether they had heard of the manager or not. All the information gleaned in this manner was statistically combined to arrive at a score which we plotted vertically on a 21-point scale. On this scale a score of 10 would indicate that 100% of the sample regarded management to be totally trustworthy; a score of -10 would indicate that 100% of the sample regarded management to be totally untrustworthy (figure 1.1).

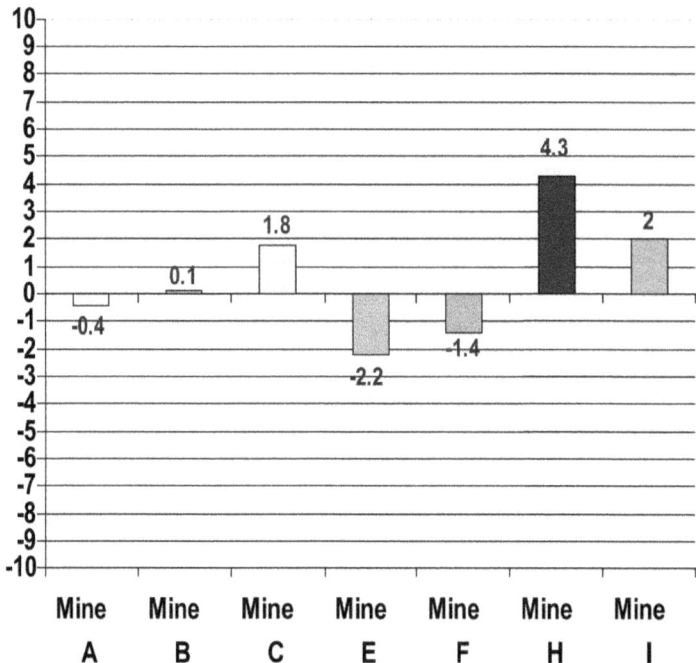

Figure 1.1 - Trust in Management on Mines A, B, C, E, F, H, I

Scores that approximated the middle of the scale would either reflect a difference of opinion across the sample or a lack of knowledge of management. Clearly, trust should not be assessed if the sample was not familiar with the body – it is impossible to trust (or distrust) something or somebody you do not know. In order to indicate whether the score approximated the middle of the scale because of a difference of opinion across the sample or because of a lack of knowledge, the knowledge component of the trust score was indicated on the hori- zontal axis.

Armed with this instrument we descended on seven mines in the industry in 1985 and 1986 to assess the climate of employee opinion. In all these studies we investigated only the opinions of black employees. This was done by means of face-to-face interviews conducted by a team of professional interviewers who could speak the various vernac- ulars of black mine workers. On each mine we interviewed a selected sample of between 200 and 300 men. (In most cases I shall not refer to a mine by its name since we were bound by a Chamber agreement not to divulge the identity of any mines on which we worked.)

On examining the trust in management on the seven mines we found the levels to be extremely variable (Figure 1.1). Trust in management on Mine H, for example was very high, whereas trust in management on Mine E was relatively poor. On the other mines trust in management fell somewhere between the extremes set by Mines H and E. These findings suggest two things:

• First, the Marxists were wrong; employees and employers are not necessarily separated by an absolute divide because it is possible for employees to trust management, even in an industry as crude as the South African gold mining industry.

• Second, it brought a question to the fore; what would explain the various levels of trust? Why did employees on one mine trust their managers while on another mine management was distrusted?

We examined the literature and also spoke to various managers in the industry to find possible explanations for the problem that we could test against the information we had gathered. We needed to establish a set of hypotheses that would account for these extraordinary findings.

The list of possible explanations turned out to be quite long but we eventually succeeded in reducing it to the following factors:

• **Physical conditions**: If people are housed in poor accommodation or have to work in difficult and dangerous circumstances they will not trust management.

• **Labour Mix**: For historical, cultural or other reasons various groups of men are differently predisposed towards the industry.

• **Rates of pay**: If people are not well paid they will not trust management.

• **Political influences**: The current local and national political debates have a direct influence on trust in management.

• **Lack of human resource function**: Without a sophisticated human resources function with its associated personnel, systems and procedures for handling staff issues ranging from pay queries to disciplinary action, employees will not trust management.

• **Trade union activity**: If a trade union is active on a site, trust in management will necessarily be poor because employees will be subjected to union propaganda. Furthermore, the union's agenda will affect the profile it maintains on site. For example, the approach of a black consciousness union towards management and employees will differ from that of a socialist union.

• **Management style**: Managers' behaviour towards employees will directly affect trust in management.

The subsequent investigation to determine which of these factors accounted for the different levels of trust on the seven mines yielded disturbing surprises. It became evident that most of the factors listed above played absolutely no role in determining trust. I would like to prove this point by examining each factor in turn.

Physical Conditions

For the purpose of this discussion I would like to refer to the conditions prevailing on Mine C at the time of the study. Mine C was the oldest operating mine in the industry, and the conditions were worse than Dickensian. Employees were housed in hostels which had been built for Chinese indentured labourers in the 1880's. Just walking through the hostels gave one the distinct impression that 19th century Chinese must have been physically minute because all the facilities in these hostels resembled nursery school furniture.

Forty men were housed in a room not much larger than the lounge of an average South African suburban home. The men slept on concrete bunks that were so short that a man of average height had no alternative but to sleep with his feet protruding beyond his bunk. Although the men were given foam mattresses to sleep on, they were only about 2cm thick – scant comfort on a cold concrete slab, particularly in the highveld winter.

One of the mine officials I spoke to claimed that the hostels had last been re-roofed in the 1930's, which I could well believe because the corrugated iron sheets were rusted through and, looking up, I could see a myriad of pinpricks of sunlight breaking through the roof. This meant that some of these roofs would leak like sieves during a thunderstorm.

Because the mine was marginal, meaning that it just managed to eke out a living at the prevailing gold price, cost cutting was the norm. Management tried to secure all supplies as cheaply as possible, including rations for the hostel dwellers. Offal, euphemistically referred to as fish, was bought from the cheapest local contractor and served twice a week. The offal was so cheap because it had not been cleaned properly, which basically meant it was still full of dung. One could literally see dung particles floating in the stew!

The underground conditions on this mine were also unbelievably poor. For more than a century the mine had grown like some subterranean amoebic infection in the bowels of the earth. In the ongoing pursuit of new ground to mine, the exposed reef became ever deeper and further removed from the main vertical shafts. This meant that it could take up to two hours just to get from the shaft to the workplace, a journey during which the worker might have to walk many kilometers underground and to be hoisted down several sub-vertical or sub-incline shafts.

The dispersed distribution and great depth of underground workings had a enormous impact on both ventilation and the stability of underground excavations. The air that was supposed to ventilate the stopes basically entered along the same meandering route as the men who worked there, past rock surfaces that could be as hot as 50ºC. Most workplaces were therefore extremely hot, men were still dying of heat stress – something that no longer occurred anywhere else in the industry. The instability of the ground made the mine very sensitive to seismic events and underground workings collapsed frequently. Fifty men died in underground accidents in 1985, and 52 in 1986.

In short, Mine C was an absolute nightmare to work on in terms of physical conditions, particularly in the case of black employees. But, the really extraordinary thing about this mine was that employee's trust in management was higher than on most other mines. On this mine men were being fed dung and got killed underground, and yet they loved their managers!

By way of contrast I would like to mention Mine E, a large consolidated operation in the Orange Free State. One of the divisions of this mine was comparatively new, and conditions there were very good. The hostels were of the most modern in the industry, with men accommodated four to a room furnished with proper bedsteads. They had access to communal lounges that were equipped with television sets and a number of other recreational activities. Because the mine was new, most workplaces were relatively close to the shafts, which meant ventilation was relatively good and workplaces were safe. The mine also had one of the best safety records in the industry. However, trust in management on this mine was poorer than on any of the other mines included in the study. In fact, a number of interviewees even threatened to necklace certain managers.

The extremes presented by these operations suggested that physical conditions did not have an impact on trust in management. This view was borne out by an examination of the physical conditions on the other mines. (table 1.1)

Table 1.1 - Trust in management related to physical conditions

Mine	Trust	Conditions	
		Work	Hostel
Mine H	4.3	-	•
Mine I	2.0	•	+
Mine C	1.8	-	-
Mine B	0.1	•	+
Mine A	-0.4	•	•
Mine F	-1.4	•	-
Mine E	-2.2	+	+

Key: - Poor, + Good, • Average.

The fact that, for example, hostels were good or workplaces were comfortable and safe had absolutely no impact on trust. I must add that we also saw poor conditions coupled with low trust, and good conditions coupled with a high level of trust, but this merely confirmed our findings that one cannot relate trust in management to the physical conditions of employees.

Labour Mix

A popular belief in the mining industry at the time held that men from the various labour supplying areas of Southern Africa responded differently to the mining experience.

Shangaans from Mozambique were considered to be the best workers; they "never got cheeky, and did as they were told". These characteristics were attributed to various factors, the most ridiculous being that they come from a tropical climate with a preponderance of diseases such as sleeping sickness, which made them slow and docile. The Sothos, on the other hand, were considered brave and hardworking (dangerous jobs such as shaft sinking were done almost exclusively by Sothos), but they were also seen as volatile and difficult to appease once aroused. Generally, however, Sothos were felt to be on the side of management and the establishment.

The men who were seen to be mainly negatively disposed towards management were the Xhosas ("Xhosa" was used generically to refer to all who came from the Eastern Cape, Ciskei and Transkei.) Pondos were considered to be the "worst" of the Xhosa group, and this contention was supported by objective evidence. Macnamara, for example, found that Pondos were more frequently involved in "communal conflict" or mobilization against other groups. In general, Xhosas were also more often involved in mobilizations against management than any other group.

The implications of all this with regard to trust in management were therefore that Shangaans always trusted management, Xhosas never did and Sothos did most of the time but not always. Therefore, if one desired to establish a climate of favourable employee opinion, the solution would be to employ many Shangaans, a couple of Sothos (to do the dangerous work) and perhaps a few Xhosas to ensure that employees' feelings of restlessness remained focused among themselves instead of being directed at management.

This may sound ridiculous, but I know of a number of instances where management pursued this line of reasoning when deciding whom to employ. In some cases human resources managers were even assigned to come up with the best formula for a labour mix - "hubble, bubble, toil and trouble"! However, this kind of alchemy almost without fail had disastrous consequences. In fact, as far as I know, it always led to endemic communal conflict which resulted in numerous deaths, disruptions in production and damage to mine facilities.

It would be possible, on the basis of evidence provided by our initial investigation into trust in management, to argue against the assumptions on which this kind of manipulation is founded. On Mine C, for example, there was only a marginal difference in the trust in management shown by Xhosas, Sothos and Shangaans (fig 1.2). However, this similarity in trust across the three groups was by no means typical of the industry. In all the climate surveys I have done on mines there was a very definite trend for Shangaans to have a high level of trust in management and for Xhosas to have a low level of trust. The level of trust of Sothos was situated somewhere between these two extremes.

This phenomenon has a historical explanation. Xhosas, for example, were recruited in large numbers after the Francistown air disaster in 1973. At that stage the largest single group of mine workers came from Malawi - a trend of which the president of Malawi, Hastings Banda, did not approve. The crash of a plane full of Malawian mine workers near Francistown in Botswana was the straw that broke the camel's back, and he ordered the immediate suspension of all recruitment of labour to South African mines. Because of the staggering numbers of Malawians employed by the industry at the time, this was potentially dangerous to mines, and the industry immediately set about finding other areas from which to recruit labour.

It would be possible, on the basis of evidence provided by our initial investigation into trust in management, to argue against the assumptions on which this kind of manipulation is founded.

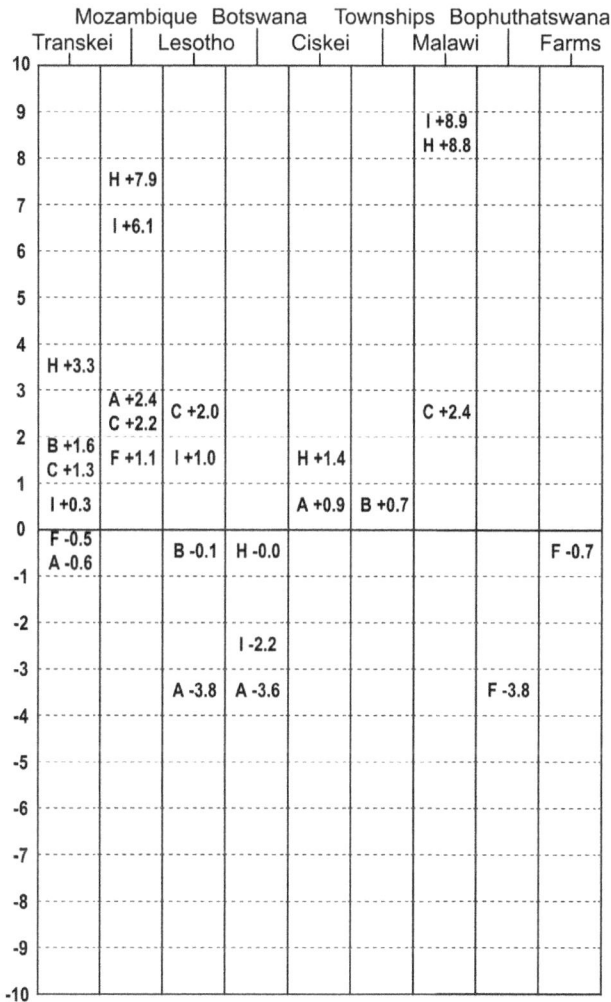

	Transkei	Mozambique Lesotho	Botswana	Townships Ciskei	Malawi	Bophuthatswana	Farms
10							
9							
8						I +8.9 / H +8.8	
7	H +7.9						
6	I +6.1						
5							
4							
3	H +3.3						
2	B +1.6 / C +1.3	A +2.4 / C +2.2 / F +1.1	C +2.0 / I +1.0			C +2.4	
1	I +0.3			H +1.4 / A +0.9	B +0.7		
0	F -0.5 / A -0.6		B -0.1	H -0.0			F -0.7
-1							
-2			I -2.2				
-3			A -3.8	A -3.6		F -3.8	
-4							
-5							
-6							
-7							
-8							
-9							
-10							

Figure 1.2 - Trust in management among men from different regions

On Mine C, for example, there was only a marginal difference in the trust in management shown by Xhosas, Sothos and Shangaans (fig 1.2). However, this similarity in trust across the three groups was by no means typical of the industry. In all the climate surveys I have done on mines there was a very definite trend for Shangaans to have a high level of trust in management and for Xhosas to have a low level of trust. The level of trust of Sothos was situated somewhere between these two extremes.

The primary area of focus was Transkei, and over the next two years the mining industry recruited large numbers of Transkeians who, because they lacked experience, were mostly appointed as unskilled workers. Soon after these Transkeians had joined the industry a major change in employment policy was implemented which had far reaching implications for all migrant mine workers.

Prior to 1973 mine workers had worked on contract, and when the contract expired they returned home for an unspecified period of time. Sometimes they stayed at home for several years before entering into another contract. Since this caused problems with regard to manpower planning, the mining industry introduced a system of valid re-engagement guarantees (VRG's) in 1974. These guaranteed an employee his job if he returned within a specified period of time.

The effect of this arrangement was that after 1974, the labour distribution on mines remained static. In other words, the young Xhosas who joined the industry during this period, entering at the bottom of the hierarchy, had their status entrenched by VRGs: they would remain juniors and their (more or less permanent) immediate supervisors would invariably be Sothos. The result was twofold: tremendous tension arose between Sothos and Xhosas, and at the same time the scene was set for resentment towards management on the part of the Xhosas for having been in effect, permanently cast as "hewers of wood and drawers of water".

The Sothos were the senior employees in 1974, and their status was equally entrenched by VRGs. They became a kind of labour aristocracy of professional miners who wore their identity wrist bands with pride. Their position also created the impression with management that they were superior workers and as a result of this prejudice, most senior positions that became vacant after 1974 were filled by Sothos. This naturally entrenched the divide between Sothos and Transkeians.

But the situation of the Shangaans was probably the most tragic of all. The civil war in Mozambique had devastated the country to such an extent that a job on the mines offered the only hope of survival for many.

I encountered many stories of Mozambicans who, upon their return to the mines after time spent at home, were so emaciated that they would draw up to four times the normal rations of non-controlled foodstuffs in a conscious attempt to fatten-up in preparation for their next "home leave". These men were certainly not going to hold opinions or engage in activities that might jeopardize their tenure on the mine.

Certain consistencies therefore existed in the distribution of levels of trust across these different groups of employees that could plausibly be explained in terms of the history of a particular group on a mine. It would be dangerous, however, to come to absolute conclusions on trust in management on this basis.

For example, while the trust shown by Shangaans as a group was generally higher than the trust shown by any other group on the same mine, the level of trust in management among Shangaans on various mines varied greatly: trust in management among Shangaans on Mine F was only marginally positive, while Shangaans on Mine H showed an extremely high degree of trust in management (fig 1.2). Similarly, the trust of Transkeians on Mine F was marginally poor, whereas it was quite positive on Mine H. In fact, Transkeians trust in the management of Mine H was higher than that of Mozambicans on Mine F.

This suggested that although Shangaans as a group tended to have a higher level of trust, this trend was so mine specific that it could not explain the problem of trust in management in any essential sense. There had to be something else, something associated with the experiences of men on the mine itself, which fundamentally accounted for trust.

Rates of Pay

One of the factors associated with men's experience of the workplace would be their remuneration. It is popularly believed that people work for money, and that they will not trust you unless you remunerated them adequately.

Mine E was a consolidated operation consisting of three divisions (fig 1.3). Identical rates of pay and conditions of service, laid down by the policy of Mine E, were applicable to each of the three divisions. Trust in management on the three divisions differed enormously, with positive trust indicated in Division 1, poor trust in Division 2 and very poor trust in Division 3.

More recently I encountered positive trust on mines that were not members of the Chamber of Mines and whose employees were paid less than others in the industry. This again shows that trust cannot be accounted for in terms of rates of pay. Whether you pay your workers the top rate for an industry or the bottom rate is immaterial and will not have any bearing on the extent to which they trust you.

The Prevailing Political Debate

There is a common feeling among many managers in South Africa that conflict at work is really rooted in the evils of apartheid, and that they can do very little about it. Unless a political settlement is reached, they claim, the workplace will remain the primary venue where black employees will vent their political frustrations. This view implies that employees do not trust management because they do not trust the broader establishment, and that it is therefore not within the power of the manager to address poor trust in management on a site.

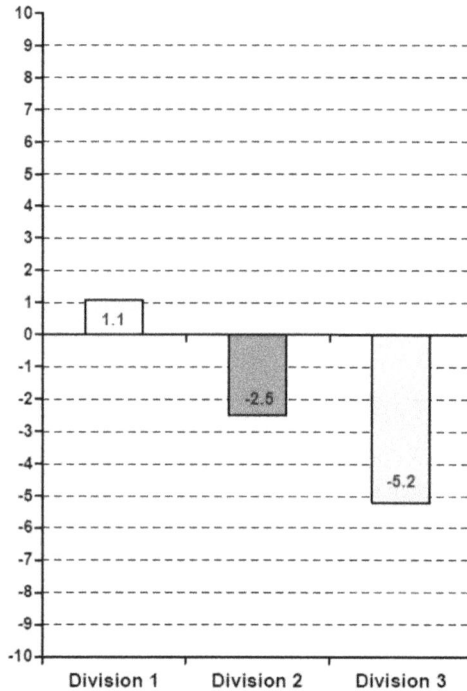

Figure 1.3 - Trust in management on MINE E, divisions 1, 2 & 3

If one were to refer again to the different levels of trust in the various divisions of Mine E, this point of view is not plausible. The entire complex of this mine is situated in one region, and employees have equal access to the local townships and therefore the wider political debate. We conducted our fieldwork in the three divisions simultaneously, which means that one must assume that the issues in the political debate at the time remained a constant factor. Yet trust in management varied from positive in one division to appalling in another. Since the political arena was identical for all three divisions, the differences in trust cannot be ascribed to political climate.

To pursue this point even further I would like to refer to Mine H, situated within walking distance of Soweto, a township that was regarded as one of the most political in the country. Workers on Mine H had close contact with township residents and spent much of their leisure time in the township. Despite this close contact with an extremely politicised community, workers on Mine H had a very high level of trust in management.

Lack of a Human Resources Function

The development of modern personnel departments in the mining industry during the 1960s, and their subsequent sophistication and expansion into a plethora of functions covering everything from communication to industrial relations portfolios, have generally been viewed as a positive contribution in addressing employee discontent and gaining employee trust.

This view gave rise to the perception (most frequently held by human resources people themselves) that it is impossible to have sound employer-employee relationships without a human resources function. Moreover, it is often believed that a human resources department in itself guarantees healthy relationships between employers and employees.

Let us refer once again to Mine E where the human resources department was similarly structured in all three divisions. This proves that the mere presence of such a department does not buy employee commitment. To make this point even more strongly, one should look at the case of Mine F which had a very well-developed human resources department that employed specialists to deal with issues ranging form welfare problems to industrial relations. Trust on this mine, however, remained poor. Mine H, on the other hand, had only a rudimentary human resources function and yet, trust there was high. Therefore, the mere presence of such a function does not account for the variance in trust between these two mines, and also does not account for the range of trust we found on all seven mines included in the initial survey.

Trade Union Involvement

In the mid-80s, when we conducted the initial surveys, mine managers regarded trade unions as a new kind of disease, an inexplicably contracted and absolutely debilitating virus that affected organisations like yuppie flu affects people. Managers generally agreed that to have a union on site was to court disaster. The only reason why they would allow a union on a mine was the pressure exerted on them by the liberals at head office in Johannesburg who were very concerned about the mining industry's poor image with regard to its treatment of people.

To have a union on site, managers felt, would be to lose all control over the workforce and to eliminate any possibility of their trusting management, since the aim of the union was to politicise employees and destroy any loyalty they might have towards management. Although this may have been perfectly true in terms of the agenda of the union, the degree to which a union can actually affect trust in management is questionable.

Trust in management on Mines C and I, for example, was very similar, despite the fact that there was virtually no union presence on Mine C and an incredibly strong one on Mine I. The relatively high trust on Mine I may also be contrasted with the lower levels of trust on Mines A, B, and F, all of which did not have as strong a union presence.

Two subsequent studies confirmed this phenomenon. At one of the shafts on Mine O there was a particularly high trust in management, despite the fact that 95% of the men were members of NUM (National Union of Mineworkers). On the other hand, I also worked on a colliery in the Eastern Transvaal where trust in management was very poor - and union involvement nil!

At the time of our initial investigation into the factors affecting trust, one mine seemed to provide evidence for the contention the unions affect trust in management, namely Mine E (see table 1.2). Trust in management on this mine was lower than on any of the other mines and it was also the most unionized of them all.

Table 1.2 - Union activity and trust in management

Mine	Trust	Union activity
Mine H	4.3	Exposure to two unions No recognition
Mine I	2.0	Union recognised
Mine C	1.8	No union activity
Mine B	0.1	Little union activity
Mine A	-0.1	Little union activity
Mine F	-1.4	Intense union activity No recognition
Mine E	-2.2	Highly unionized

However these facts should be viewed in their proper context: the union played an equally prominent role in all three divisions of the mine, whereas trust in management on the divisions, as I pointed out before, varied greatly.

There is however, further information relating to Mine E that sheds important light on the problem of trust in management and the degree to which it is influenced by union involvement. This information was brought to light by what we called the problem-solving roles technique.

The problem-solving roles technique is a simple but effective diagnostic instrument that enables one to identify the kind of roles employees appeal to for sympathetic attention when experiencing a work-related problem. Subjects are provided with a list of both formal and informal roles that are typical of the operation, and are then asked to identify those that would be sympathetic to a work related problem. A gold mine has on average 18 such roles. We would count the positive responses to each of these roles, in order to arrive at a ranking. Table 1.3 lists the six most sympathetic roles in the three divisions of Mine E.

On examining this table it is clear that the role of union representative was one of the most important, if not the most important in resolving work-related problems in all three divisions. Despite the fact that the union was equally important in the three divisions, trust in management varied, indicating that the variance could not be ascribed to the profile of the union representative. Rather, the variance among the divisions could be associated with a variance in the degree to which other roles, and more specifically roles associated with the hierarchy of the mine, were seen to be important.

In Division 1, where trust in management was highest, all six the most important roles were appealed to by more than 70% of the workforce.

Table 1.3 - Ranking of roles (MINE E) sympathetic to
work-related problems

Division 1		Division 2		Division 3	
Role	%	Role	%	Role	%
Union representative	98	Co-Worker	95	Union representative	94
Personnel assistant	92	Team Leader	95	Co-Worker	90
Team leader	90	Union representative	90	Team Leader	68
Co-worker	88	Personnel assistant	78	Personnel assistant	64
Committee representative	86	Home Friend	70	Shift boss	52
Shift boss	74	White D.P.O*	68	Room mate	48

(*D.P.O. - Departmental Personnel O'cer)

Four of these roles were formal and one, that of shift boss, was a white, line, supervisory role. This means that, while the union representative was the most important sympathetic role in this division, his was regarded in the same light as many other roles associated with management.

In Division 2, where trust was poorer than in division 1, the union representative remained important, although in this case only two formal management roles were regarded as sympathetic by more than 70% of the men, and both these roles were black (the team leader and the personnel assistant).

In Division 3, too, the union representative was important, but none of the formal roles associated with the hierarchy of the mine was regarded as sympathetic.

Thus, while the degree to which the union was seen to be sympathetic did not account for trust, the degree to which roles associated with the line of command were seen to be sympathetic had a direct bearing on trust. This suggests that a key factor in accounting for trust in management is associated with the behaviour of management representatives.

Management Style

The importance of management style in determining trust in management was first suggested by the results of four surveys done on mines C, F, H and I. One of the questions was: Do you feel that relations with management have improved, stayed good, stayed bad or deteriorated over the last two to three years?" (See table 1.4)

In the next question, employees were asked to give reasons for their answers. On all four mines, the men who said that relations with management had improved, believed it was because management had attended to grievances (raised 122 times) and also because there were committees that served to represent workers to management (raised 10 times).

Table 1.4 - Employee perceptions of relations with management

Mine	Improved %	Stayed good %	Stayed bad %	Deterio rated %
Mine C	22	48	25	5
Mine F	19	36	36	9
Mine H	25	40	32	3
Mine I	22	45	23	16
Average	22	43	28	7

Since the aim of these committees was to address employee problems, the second reason cited was in fact closely associated with the first. In other words, all employees who felt relations with management had improved basically said that this was so because management had attended to grievances.

The men who felt that relations with management had remained good, ascribed it to the fact that they had had no complaints (raised 141 times), that management had attended to grievances (raised 112 times), that management treated employees like human beings (raised 21 times) and that management did not bother or harass employees (raised 10 times).

The two most frequent responses, i.e. of not having had complaints and of grievances having been attended to, were related because if one has no complaints it means whatever grievances one might have had, had been attended to. Management's handling of grievances was therefore a primary issue with men who felt relations with management had remained good. Even the response of being treated like human beings commented on the way grievances were handled, as evidenced by the following comment form an employee on Mine E: "Management takes employee problems seriously; they see the importance of employees on the mine."

Employees who said that relations with management had remained bad believed this was because management did not attend to grievances (raised 132 times), wages were inadequate (raised 36 times), and management discriminated against blacks (raised 23 times). Not having one's grievances attended was actually seen as central to being discriminated against and not being treated as a human being. This was voiced by a man who said: "Employee problems are piling up and the mine does nothing to solve them. Management thinks employees are cattle, they think they can do what they like."

Clearly, the central issue raised by employees who felt relations with management had stayed bad was that management had not attended to grievances. The same was true for men who felt relations with management had deteriorated - 29 of them indicated that this was because management had not attended to grievances. No other issues were raised to any degree of importance by these employees.

In all four of the categories of response, management's handling of grievances was the primary reason raised as motivation for the response. This implies that the way in which grievances were handled was a central criterion in terms of which management was assessed. This key criterion was applied irrespective of whether the assessment was positive or negative.

The next question of interest to us with regard to this criterion was whether it held any implication with regard to trust in management. On one of the mines (Mine E) we asked a very simple question: "Do you think grievance procedures on this mine are effective or ineffective?" Of the total sample interviewed, 58% felt that these procedures were ineffective, and 42% felt they were effective. The trust in management across these two groups varied enormously (fig 1.4).

Men who felt grievance procedures were effective had a positive trust in management (+3.5). Those who thought grievance procedures were ineffective had a particularly negative trust in management (-6.3). This again suggested that the issue of grievance handling was used as a central criterion to assess management - in this instance, to determine whether trust in the manager was granted or withheld.

Figure 1.4 - Trust in management among men who regarded grievance procedures to be effective/ineffective

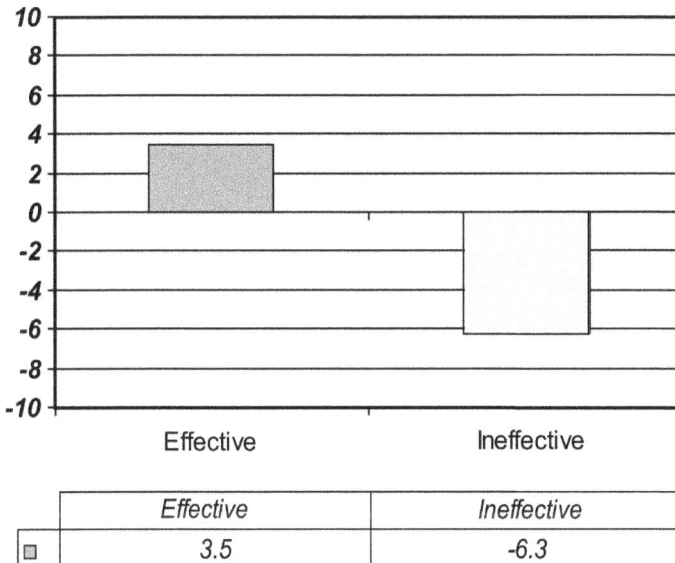

	Effective	Ineffective
☐	3.5	-6.3

This particular finding was very exciting, and prompted us to examine whether the results from the other six mines in our initial survey reflected a similar trend. Unfortunately, the question whether grievance procedures were effective was not asked as such in these other surveys, but a very similar one was included: "Is management interested in the welfare of employees?" If the manager had an interest in employee welfare, he would naturally attend to their problems.

The question was structured, and allowed for two possible answers, yes or no. The men who responded positively we dubbed the positive group, and those who responded negatively we referred to as the negative group (table 1.5).

Table 1.5 - Management interest in employee welfare on six mines

Mine	A	B	C	F	H	I
% Yes	50	60	52	44	70	60
% No	50	40	48	56	30	40

A cursory examination of the results revealed a relationship between overall trust in management and the size of the so-called positive and negative groups. On mine H, which had the highest trust in management, the positive group accounted for 70% of the sample, whereas the negative group was relatively small at 30%. On mine F, which had the lowest level of trust, the positive group was small (44% of the sample) while the negative group was large (56%). Therefore, where the positive group was large, overall trust in management was high, and where the negative group was big, overall trust in management was poor.

Furthermore, we investigated the trust in management of every positive and negative group on every mine (fig 1.5). In each case we found that men who felt that management had an interest in employee welfare had a positive trust in management, whereas those who felt management was not interested in employee welfare had a low level of trust in management. In other words, management was accepted or rejected on the strength of their perceived interest in their employees, and trust was granted or withheld on this basis. Showing an interest in employees when approached with a problem thus served as a criterion for judging a manger. If he lived up to these expectations he was trusted. If he did not he was distrusted.

Another interesting relationship came to the fore: the relative size of either the positive or negative group on a mine and its trust in management. On Mine H for example, the positive group accounted for 70% of the sample, and its trust in management was higher than the trust of the smaller positive groups on any other mines. Also, the trust of the relatively small negative group on Mine H was less negative than the trust of the negative groups on any of the other mines. By contrast, the trust of the large negative group on Mine F was lower than the trust of all the other negative groups; the trust of the small positive group on this mine was less positive then that of the positive groups on the other mines. This suggested that the difference in trust in management between the positive and negative groups remained reasonably consistent (around 8 points on the trust scale).

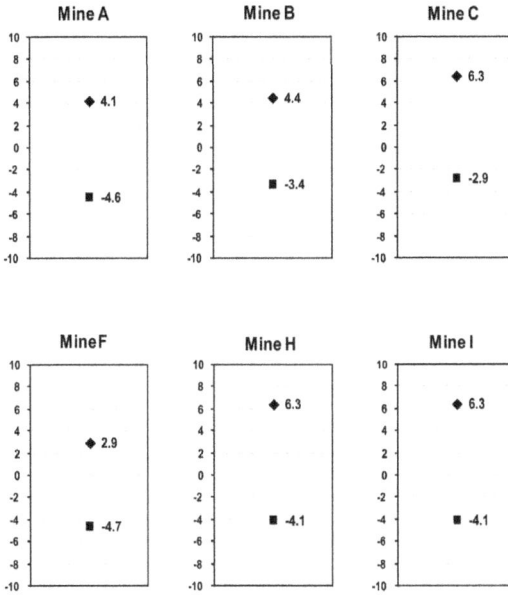

Figure 1.5 - Trust in management in relation to management's
perceived interest in employee welfare

However, the distribution of the trust scores for both these groups was related to the size of either group. If the positive group was relatively large, trust in management for both groups would be more positive, whereas if the negative group was relatively large the trust of both groups would be lower.

The next question we asked ourselves was whether this criterion was used only to measure trust in senior management, or also to assess other roles in the hierarchy of the mine. One of the roles for which we assessed trust in these six surveys was that of the (white) supervisor, i.e. the miner or shift boss (fig. 1.6)

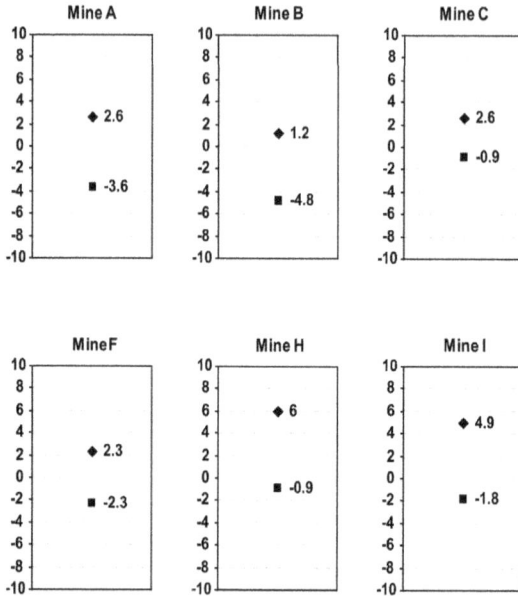

Figure 1.6 - Trust in white supervisors in relation to management's perceived interest in employee welfare

We found that men who felt management was interested in their welfare had a much higher trust in the supervisor than those who felt management had no such interest. In other words, not only did management stand or fall by the criterion of attending to people's welfare, so did the supervisor.

The same yardstick was used to assess both manger and supervisor. There was, however, one important difference: although the white supervisor stood or fell according to these terms, he did not stand or fall as absolutely as did the manager. As far as supervisors were concerned, the difference between positive and negative groups was smaller. We therefore concluded that although the same criterion was used to assess both manager and senior supervisor/middle manager it was not used to the same extent.

Pursuing this line of reasoning even further, we found the same to be true for immediate supervisors or team leaders (fig. 1.7). The employees who felt that management was interested in their welfare trusted their immediate supervisors significantly more than men who believed management to have no interest in this regard.

Although even negative groups showed positive trust in their immediate supervisor, one should not read to much into this because, as far these six studies were concerned, trust in the team leader was the most predictable factor.

Regardless of the mine, region of origin of employees or job category, trust in the team leader always measured around 6 points. The only difference lay in employees' perceptions of whether management took an interest in their welfare or not. Those who believed management to be interested in their welfare were far more likely to trust the team leader.

We did notice, however, that as far as the immediate supervisor was concerned, the difference in trust was even less extreme than in the case of the white supervisor. This indicates a telescopic effect, i.e. the further down the hierarchy a role is situated, the less stringently criteria are applied in its assessment.

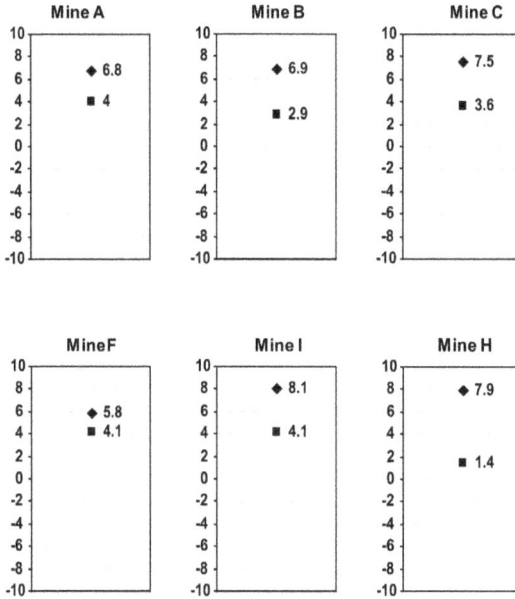

Figure 1.7 - Trust in team leaders in relation to management's
perceived interest in employee welfare

To summarise: first, the employee judged the manager in terms of very simple criteria, namely whether the manager had a genuine interest in the welfare of the employee. Secondly, the further down the hierarchy the manager and the less powerful he was, the less stringently this criterion was imposed. Conversely, the more powerful the manager was, the more absolutely the criterion was imposed.

These findings suggest a relationship between the criteria people use to judge their managers and power. In fact, it is evident that the criteria used by employees to evaluate management are the same as those used to measure power. When this connection first dawned on us at the Human Resources Laboratory we were actually quite shocked - it seemed quite unbecoming for a group of liberal social scientists to arrive at such a conclusion.

However, when you look at it again, it is not altogether surprising that there is a relationship between the criteria that workers use to judge their managers and power. In fact, power is the name of the game in the workplace. When a manager or supervisor instructs a subordinate to do something, he is exercising his power. These criteria demonstrate that there is nothing inherently wrong with instructing someone to do something, to deliver, when exercising power. It is nothing to get upset about, or feel guilty about. However, no manager has the right to exercise power simply on the basis of rank, or because he has paid a wage, or for any other arbitrary reason. You only have the right to ask someone to do something, to "deliver", if you care.

Bearing this in mind another very important consequence comes to the fore. Take a look at the substantial difference in trust between the positive and negative groups with regards to the black supervisor at Mine H (the high trust mine). This difference implies that on Mine H, the criterion in terms of which power was measured was imposed relatively stringently on the first line supervisor. One could confirm this by looking at the kinds of decision a supervisor could take. He could deal with any problem, from cash advances to unpaid leave. It therefore seems that there is a relationship between high trust in management and the degree to which the supervisor is empowered to look after his subordinates.

Mine F demonstrates the reverse: trust in management was the lowest of the six mines under discussion, and the difference in trust between the positive and negative groups was extremely small with regard to the black supervisor. In other words, the criterion in terms of which power is measured, was hardly used to judge the black supervisor on Mine F. In fact, the black supervisor was regarded as nothing more than another good black college, and not as a representative of management, of power. This means that management was not trusted in a situation where the immediate supervisor was not seen to be powerful.

This pattern of response makes sense in view of the point we made that the criteria according to which an employee judges management have to do with power. It is not up to a general manager sitting at the top of the organisation to exercise power, he does not give instructions to the worker on the floor. The supervisor is the one who gives instructions, he is the one who exercises power. If the supervisor is not equipped to deal with problems brought to him by a subordinate, the power exercised by the supervisor will be regarded as illegitimate, because it will not have the effect that power is supposed to have, it will not do for the people what it is meant to do.

Furthermore, it is not only the power of the supervisor that will be regarded as illegitimate, but the power of the entire organisation. This does not mean that people will distrust the supervisor *per se*. On the contrary, it is easy to trust a powerless supervisor because he is an equal, he has no authority. But, it is only the powerful supervisor who can *earn* trust for the organisation and its leadership.

The next question we wanted to investigate was whether these criteria were imposed only in the workplace, or across a broader spectrum. We discovered that the criteria did not affect only the organisation, but a whole group of institutions associated with the establishment (figs 1.8, 1.9, 1.10). In other words, if an employee standing on a site asked himself whether management had an interest in his welfare, and decided that the answer the answer was "no", he did not only write off management in his mind, but also head office, the South African government and even his home government if he came from, for example Lesotho or Transkei. On the other hand, if his answer were "yes", he would not only affirm management at the same time, but also all associated institutions.

At first glance these views may strike one as being extremely naive. However, on careful consideration they are revealed as very astute. Our whole Southern African establishment is about power, and the focus of that power, the place where it actually finds expression, is the workplace.

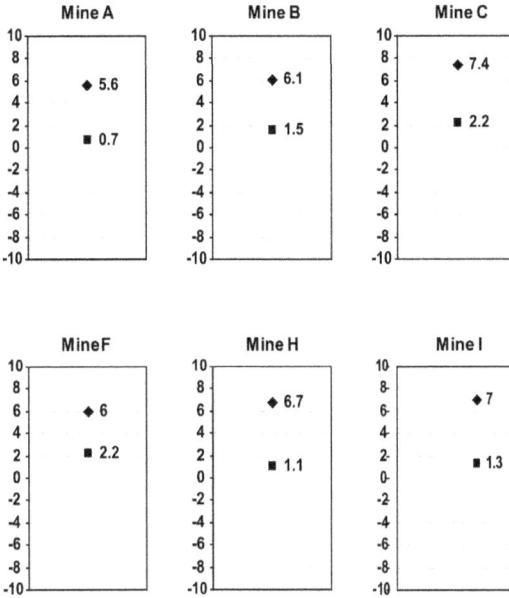

Figure - 1.8 Trust in head offce in relation to management's
perceived interest in employee welfare

It is at work where people have to submit routinely to the power exercised by someone else, when they are told by someone else what to do. In fact, the workplace is far more consequential than any other place. If a policeman in the street would appropriate for himself the rights normally granted to an employer and tell you to do something for him, you would seriously question the legitimacy of his instruction.

In other words, the primary site of power in an industrial society is the workplace, because that is where people have to submit routinely to the power exercised by another. If power is not legitimate in the workplace, it will not be legitimate anywhere else.

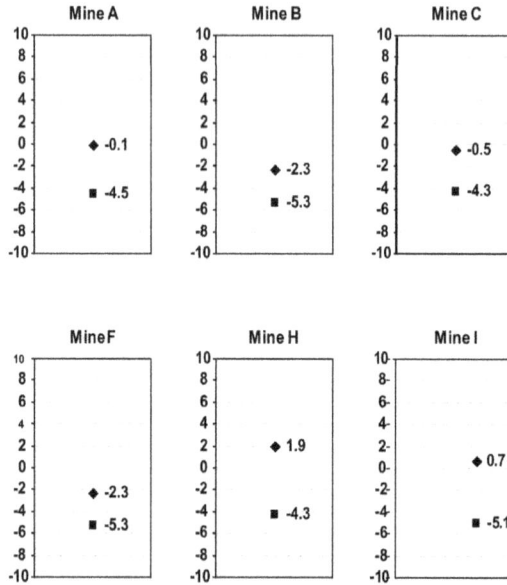

Figure - 1.9 Trust in central government in relation to
management's perceived interest in employee welfare

This sheds interesting light on our current political debate. We have all come to accept that the legitimacy of our establishment has something to do with giving disenfranchised blacks the vote, and that addressing the issue is the responsibility of politicians. The bad news is that the only thing politicians can offer us is theatre. If the power that people are actually submitted to, i.e. the power of their managers at work, is not legitimate, the establishment as a whole will remain illegitimate, whether Verwoerd or Mandela is at the helm.

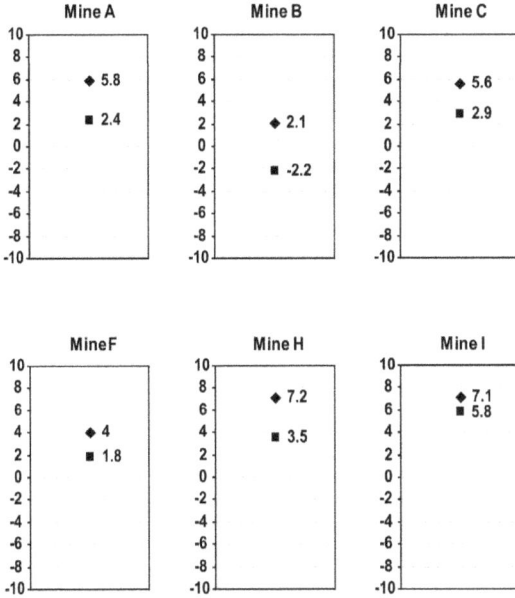

Figure 1.10 - Trust in homeland government in relation to
management's perceived interest in employee welfare

One may be tempted to dispute the relevance of these findings by arguing that all our research was done on migrant black mine workers. This is not the case. We subsequently did numerous studies of this nature at various sites, and have found the same to hold true in every instance.

In 1990 we did a survey at Safripol, for example, and we came to exactly the same conclusions. Safripol is a capital intensive producer of plastics that employs only sophisticated urbanites. In fact the majority of their workforce was white. Yet, these employees used exactly the same criterion to grant or withhold trust in management as the migrant labourer on a mine (fig 1.11).

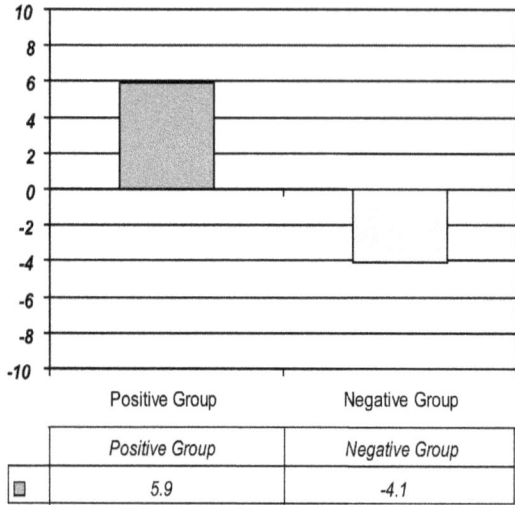

	Positive Group	Negative Group
☐	5.9	-4.1

Figure 1.11 - Trust in management at Safripol

Chapter 3

SURROGATE MANAGMENT

In chapter 1 we found that the criteria in terms of which trust is generated or withheld are related to power, and if the person who exercises the power i.e. the supervisor, does not look after his people, they will not trust management. This finding has serious implications for the way that employee discontent is generally addressed.

Usually, the corporate leadership becomes aware of the fact that the relationship between management and employee is not what it should be and that it needs to be remedied. Management then engage the services of an expert (in human resources or perhaps communications) to assist them in dealing with this problem and to pacify the people on the floor and reassure them that management does in fact care for their well-being.

The workers on the plant hear this message, they are exposed to the services of the human resources people and they learn all about how important they are from the mission statement. However, as far as they are concerned management (=power) does not care for them because the person who exercises power (their supervisor) does not care about them. The reason he does not care about them is because he believes that caring for them is not his job. He is not concerned with them; his only concern is with production, with getting units out of the door.

Even if he should be one of those remarkable people who, out of the goodness of their hearts actually want to answer for them, it will make no difference because he does not have the authority to do so. There are all sorts of people in the system whose job is to care, such as the human resources officer or the shop steward.

In most organisations with which I am familiar, management would be far more inclined to attend to a problem of a subordinate if it is presented by a shop steward than if it is brought to their attention by the employee's own supervisor. So the message the employee gets from the human resources manager *et al.* is that management cares for him, that his interests are in fact attended to and that he should therefore not burn down the plant.

But what he actually *knows* is that "power" does not care for him because the one who exercises that power, his supervisor, does not care. Although he may be hearing that management and their people say they care, his personal experience is that they do not. We all know that one would rather believe one's own experience than that which other people are trying to tell one. The worker on the floor therefore concludes that the sweet talk of the mission statement and the human resources officer is nothing more than propaganda. The danger in all this is that once an employee starts feeling this way he becomes irrevocably cynical: he has heard it all and, quite frankly, he is not about to be taken in.

We have coined a wonderful derogatory term to describe this propagandaism: "surrogate management". By surrogate management we understand the employing of a specialist, secondary or proxy function to deal with the human problem, in order to leave leadership free to pursue the business of maximising profits. In the mining industry, the manager would say: "My job is dust and holes", i.e. a technical activity. The human being becomes the concern of someone or something else.

Thus we have burgeoning personnel departments, soupedup management communication interventions, management visibility programmes, disciplinary and grievance procedures and unions. Before we examine in detail how these various surrogates are unable to address the problem of employee discontent, it may be expedient to investigate the mentality that lies in employing surrogates.

First, the surrogate is employed in the same way that drugs are administered to an ailing patient. This implies that the business plagued by discontent is perceived as an organisation that is malfunctioning (like a machine with a broken part). Therefore we call in a specialist mechanic to diagnose the problem and administer the appropriate remedy so that the malfunctioning machine will once again be able to produce. In other words, wealth is the product of a technical process, and when something is wrong, it means that the system's nuts are loose.

Let us take a look at a mine manger at work. He has a timber yard headed by a clerk through whom he draws X units of timber, and he has a store administered by another clerk from whom he gets Y units o machinery. He also has a hostel run by a *masiza,* from whom he gets Z units of labour. He mixes all these components together in terms of a formula he was taught at university, throws them down a hole and out comes gold. This is alchemy.

In the Middle Ages we would have had the good sense to burn such a man at the stake because we would have recognised that he was evil. Today we put him in charge of people since we no longer recognise the inherent wickedness of reducing people to the status of objects that can be manipulated at will. They are his tools, his human resources, the things he uses, that he employs. They are not people.

This fool cannot know what every good mine manager must know, namely that, ultimately, the rock is brought to the surface by courageous, disciplined men who have the will to go into dangerous places an blast it out. What produces the gold, then, are the generous and noble qualities of the human will. What builds wealth is the fact that a group of people are interacting in such a way that they are producing something bigger than the total of that which each individual is taking from the system. In other words, wealth is created by people who are generous, who give more than they take. Wealth is not the function of a well-designed organisation.

When the under-performing manager insists on employing human resource tinkerers and *muti* to address the problem of his unwilling subordinates, he is actually handing over to a third party the responsibility of legitimising the power he exercises. This attempt is doomed to failure, since power only gains legitimacy when the one who exercises it really cares for his subordinate. This task cannot be given to someone else because all it amounts to then is a proverbial washing of the hands in innocence.

The Personnel Function

I established my view on the role of the personnel function while trying to account for the difference in trust in management on two mines, Mine F and Mine H (fig.2.1).

Trust on Mine F was very poor; on Mine H it was very good. Mine F boasted an astonishing array of formal personnel roles that men found to be sympathetic to work-related problems (table 2.1), including a personnel assistant (masiza), a departmental personnel officer, an industrial relations officer, a social worker and a hostel manager. Among this battery of personnel types only one line role was regarded as sympathetic - the team leader. Management on Mine F had therefore spent a massive amount of money to provide an extensive personnel infrastructure to deal with employee problems, yet trust in management remained poor.

Mine H, on the other hand , had fewer roles that were regarded as sympathetic, but these were almost exclusively line roles, includingthe team leader, the miner and the shift boss. Only one strictly personnel role, the *masiza*, was regarded as sympathetic. We therefore found a high response to personnel-type roles coupled with poor trust in management on Mine F, and a high response to line roles coupled with positive trust in management on Mine H.

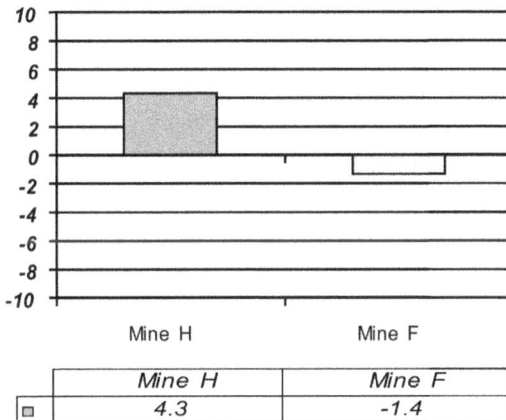

	Mine H	Mine F
▫	4.3	-1.4

Figure 2.1 - Trust in management on mines H and F

In view of the fact that the criteria used to grant or withhold trust in management are actually criteria of power, this particular pattern of response is simple to interpret.

The personnel department is not responsible for exercising power in the workplace, they do not issue instructions or maintain discipline underground. On Mine F members of the personnel department were therefore not in the position to earn trust on behalf of the men who issued instructions, despite the fact that the personnel department was regarded as effective and sympathetic in their handling of grievances. However, on Mine H, where trust in management was high, it was the line functionaries, i.e. those who were exercising power, who were seen to be looking after the people on the floor.

Mine F		Mine H	
Role	**%**	**Role**	**%**
Personnel assistant	86	Team Leader	93
Co-worker	86	Co-Worker	90
Departmental personnel	77	Personnel assistant	88
Team Leader	77	Shift Boss	83
Black Social Worker	77	Miner	80
Black Internal Relations Offcer	74	Committee Representative	73
Hostel manager	71	Departmental personnel Offcer	68
Committee Representative	70	Home Friend	61

Table 2.1 - Ranking of roles regarded as sympathetic to work-related problems on Mines F and H

One concludes then that managing people is an exercise of power that is successful only to the degree to which that power is acknowledged to be legitimate. This legitimacy is established when those who exercise power also care for and look after their subordinates. Caring for subordinates cannot be delegated to a third party, such as the personnel department.

Mr. Willie Smart, then manager of Vaal Reefs South, once told me a very interesting story that illustrated this point. There was a fatality on 8 Shaft. An inebriated employee who had been sleeping in a haulage was suddenly woken up by the sound of an approaching loco. Startled, the poor man leapt up and ran in front of the loco which, obviously flattened him. When he went to inspect the accident, Mr Smart asked the team leader if the deceased had been habitually drunk. "Yes," replied the team leader. "Then why didn't you do something about it?" Smart asked him. "I did," retorted the team leader indignantly – "I reported the matter to the masiza" (personnel assistant).

A more serious consequence of a high-profile personnel depart- ment is that the lower level operatives become notoriously corrupt. In most of the climate investigations I have done on mines, allegations were made that *masizas* are bribed into dispensing favours which involve anything from changing selection test results to organising compassionate leave.

The reason for this is that the *masiza* does not have to exercise power over people, he does not need to impose his will on others to get a job done. At the same time, however, he is structurally placed in a position where he has tremendous control over the dispensing of privileges. Since he is not in need of an employee's obedience or loyalty, exercising this control over resources quickly becomes a means for obtaining material rewards.

I have seen similar situations in the defense force. The more controls are placed in the hands of service functionaries, the more corrupt they tend to become. This is particularly true of the point of contact where the service functionary meets the one who is served. In the days of influx control, for example, the most notoriously corrupt bureaucrats were the clerks who dealt directly with the black public. They had at their disposal the battery of stamps that could mean the difference security and disaster. It was a simple matter to set up the conditions that would guide the hand to the right stamp.

All these examples serve to demonstrate two points about surrogate service functionaries such as the personnel department. First, these functionaries multiply profusely wherever those in command equip a secondary person, who does not form part of the hierarchy of command, with control. The principal aim of employing this secondary function is therefore to exercise control.

Second, these controllers are (almost) invariably associated with reprehensible and pathological behaviour. This view is probably too harsh since one cannot generalise to the extent that one would describe all employees associated with the personnel department as corrupt. However, it does attest to the essential dishonesty involved in engaging the services of a white coated human specialist to look after and pacify the workers so that those in command are free to continue exercising an illegitimate relationship of power.

This raises the question of whether there is any role for a personnel department at all, and if so, what this role should entail. In pursuit of answers to these questions, let us examine what could be a typical way of dealing with an employee's problem on a South African gold mine. (See fig. 2.2).

Let us assume that an employee receives a TEBA message that his wife has been run down by a bus in Teyateyaneng in Lesotho. He would take the message to the personnel assistant (*masiza*) because it is considered to be the job of the *masiza* to exercise control over and handle the administration of leave. The *masiza* would fill in the leave form, take it to the mine overseer for a decision and, assuming leave is granted, he would immediately inform the employee who would then leave for home.

The very last person to learn of the events would be the employee's team leader, who would only hear about it the next morning when the employee does not report for duty.

In theory and at best his miner would tell him, but more likely than not he would only discover the facts some time after having initiated disciplinary proceedings against the worker for being absent without leave. This whole process diminishes the stature of the team leader because he is not in a position to do anything for his people, and yet he has to answer for their output.

Figure 2.2 - The role of the personnel department in addressing employee problems on a typical gold mine

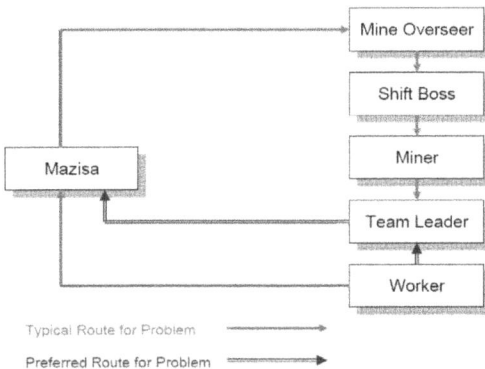

Typical Route for Problem

Preferred Route for Problem

Clearly, the decision to grant leave or not should lie with the team leader, but this would require a total reversal of routes and procedures. The team leader should have control over the leave form. From the team leader upwards, the leave form should be ratified by as few higher line functions as possible, ending with the personnel assistant whose function in this regard should be no more than record keeping. This approach would essentially reduce the role of the personnel functionary to a purely clerical one - probably to the utter horror of the human resources department.

The *masiza* could, however be given a somewhat more prestigious role. Let us refer once more to our hypothetical example:

Let us assume that the worker returns from Lesotho in a state of personal turmoil because of the death of his wife. Unable to come to terms with his loss, he starts drinking heavily and is frequently drunk on shift. The team leader knows that this man used to be an exemplary worker and consequently does not want to dismiss him forthright. However, he clearly cannot allow the new situation to continue. Ideally there should be someone in the organisation - such as the personnel functionary - to whom the team leader could turn to for advice on how to resolve the problem.

In other words, the role of he human resources functionary should not be to look after employees on behalf of line functionaries, but to assist line functionaries in looking after their people themselves.

This shows that the personnel function has a very definite, legit- imate role to fulfill: assisting line functionaries in dealing with employee concerns. However, as soon as the role of the personnel function is seen to be dealing with the problem itself rather than rendering assistance to the line function in this regard, the effect is an emasculating of lower-level line supervisors.

Management Communications

Yet another example of surrogate management is the concern with communications from management, which certainly was a fashionable way for business leaders to address employee discontent in the 80s. Even a very cursory examination will reveal that management communications constitute yet another example of surrogacy: a manager who resorts to a "communication intervention" to deal with his employees is implicitly saying that he can talk himself out of a difficult spot. This amounts to nothing more than glossing over a rotten relationship with sweet talk. It cannot work, for the same reason that any other surrogate intervention cannot work. Ultimately, the manager is seen to be voicing a concern that does not feature in the day-to-day working life of the employee. In other words, the manager appears to be lying.

Still, the issue of management communication should not be arbitrarily dismissed. In the course of our work, our understanding of this issue has gone through periods of radical review because of some of the astonishing results were obtained from our investigations.

We were convinced at the outset that management really did not have much to lose; in fact it could only gain by being seen to be talking to employees. This was the view we held at the time of our first investigation into management communications on a mine in the Orange Free State in 1986.

Management on this mine shared our conviction and had put a lot of effort into communicating with their people, inter alia by means of videos (produced in their own studio) and newsletters. Videos featuring managers speaking about various (mostly contentious) issues were shown throughout the hostel.

To our astonishment we found that the men who had seen a manager on one of these videos trusted management less than those who had never seen a manager (fig. 2.3) To add to our confusion we found that the men who read the mines newsletter trusted management whereas those who did not distrusted management. (Fig.2.4).

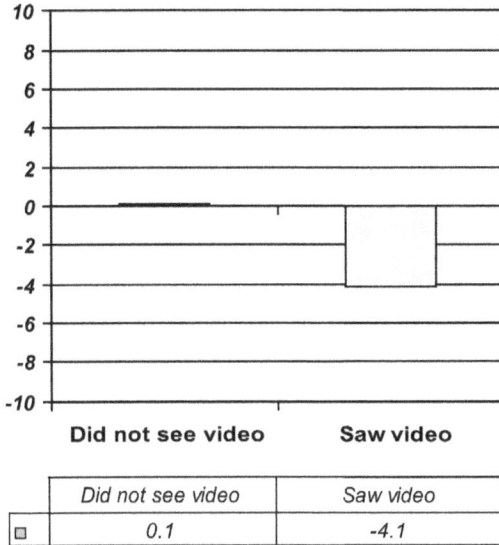

	Did not see video	Saw video
□	0.1	-4.1

Figure 2.3 - The influence of in-house videos on trust in management among men on Mine E

Figure 2.4 - The influence of newsletters on trust in management among men on mine E

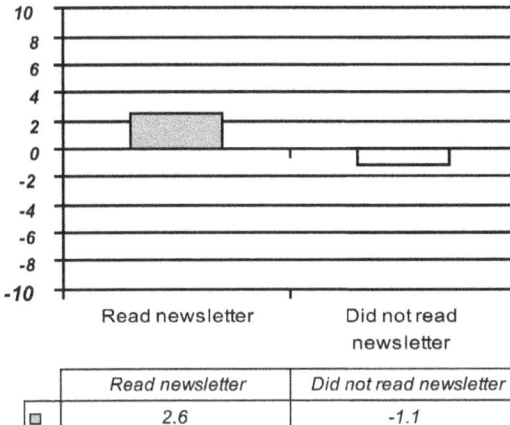

	Read newsletter	Did not read newsletter
□	2.6	-1.1

This landed us with a very interesting but thorny problem: Why was exposure to the one source associated with poor trust and exposure to the other with high trust?

My boss, Volker Hooyberg, agonised over this problem for weeks, until he came across the following line of Shakespeare: "It speaks, yet says nothing." This was the key that unlocked the explanation to the problem.

The video is a poor medium precisely because although it speaks, it does not say much. It is by nature, a "razzmatazz" medium. Producing a video is such a highly technical operation that the target audience - particularly if it is a semiliterate one - very easily feel that they are being subjected to propaganda. The video is regarded as a ploy involving management's technological edge to get the recipient to swallow contentious information. ("Just a spoonful of sugar makes the medicine go down!")

The crux of the matter is that the video is poorly equipped to fulfill the basic function of communication, i.e. imparting information. The aim is of speech, for example, is not just to make a noise (however pleasurable this may be!), but also to convey content from the speaker to the listener.

However, content is useful to the listener only if it is truthful. Therefore, content is an ethical issue because we assess it in terms of its truthfulness.

Because of its transience the video is highly unlikely to be perceived as a credible source of information. "Now you see it, now you don't."

That is the nature of information conveyed by video; you cannot store it under your bed and take it out on a later occasion to test its validity against other sources. (This is particularly true if a contentious message is conveyed.) A newsletter, on the other hand, can be stored and later retrieved to check information.

We approached the gold mining industry with the following rec- ommendation based on this interpretation. If you have a problem and need to communicate, you should bear in mind the content is the central concern in communication and that content has to do with truth. So speak the truth. In the second place, do not go overboard on media since this is both expensive and futile. The key points are that what you have to say should be true and it must also be possible to check that it is indeed the truth. Our rule of thumb therefore was: speak the truth, keep it simple and put it in writing.

What we had to say at the time made sense to a number of people, including the management of a mine that had decided that in lieu of adapting technology, large numbers of men would be retrenched. These managers knew the retrenchments would result in an industrial relations problem.

They thought they would pre-empt this problem by putting the truth in writing. Twice a week for six months they distributed a brief signed by the mine manager basically informing employees that they could expect to be retrenched. The employee would find this frightening message on his bed upon returning to the hostel having completed his shift.

The effect of this was devastating. Trust in management plummeted from marginally negative in 1986 to absolutely negative in 1987 (fig. 2.5). The only sources of information that were used by more than 50% of the workforce were associated with unions. The brief that was being pumped into the hostel twice a week was being read by only 44% of the men (table 2.2).

Table 2.2 - Ranking of useful sources of information on Mine A
in 1987

Mine A	
Role	%
Union meeting	64
Union representative	60
Co-worker	47
Written brief	44
Committee representative	28
Black supervisor	17
Signs	1.7
Notice Boards	1.4
Mine Newsletter	13
Public Address System	11

The poorest source of communication used by management was the public address system in the hostel to which only 11% of men paid any attention. This hardly came as a surprise since the public address system was used daily to announce the long litany of company numbers and names of people who had to report to the hostel manager's office for their severance packages. No wonder men were ignoring it by and large - it was the harbinger of doom.

Figure 2.5 - Trust in management on mine A in 1985 and 1987 respectively

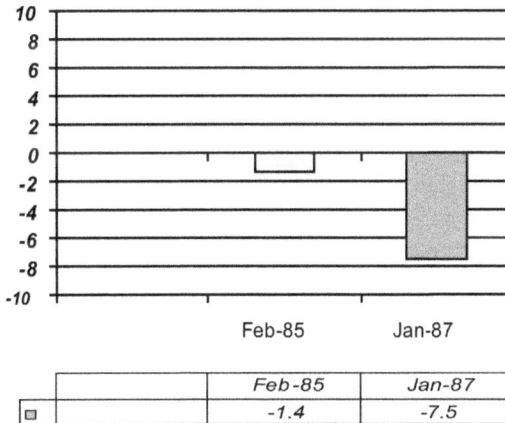

	Feb-85	Jan-87
	-1.4	-7.5

As could be expected, along with this total withdrawal from paying attention to formal media, most men felt that management was totally untrustworthy. These managers had heeded our advice: they had spoken the truth and put it in writing - with disastrous effect. However, on careful examination this is hardly surprising.

Let us assume your grandmother, whom you adore, is sitting next to you, chatting. Let us also assume you are not a major beneficiary in her will. Suddenly, a livid man bursts into the room with a wild look in his eye, frothing at the mouth and a .38 in his hand, screaming that he is going to kill your granny. The man's obvious truthfulness in this matter will most certainly not be a recipe for trust between the two of you!

Speaking the truth, let alone putting it in writing, is hardly a foolproof way of earning loyalty and trust. At this point we realised that there was something else in the issue of management communications that we had yet to discover.

Just what this "secret ingredient" was, became apparent in the course of a fascinating climate survey we did on Vaal Reefs West on the 1987 wage review strike. This was a unique opportunity, since we were conducting interviews on the mine immediately prior to the strike. We had been at it for a week when the strike started, and we had to withdraw from the mine for the ensuing three weeks. The day the men returned to work, however, was the day we resumed our interviews. In this way we gained a very important perspective on employee opinion before and after a strike. The relevant information refers specifically to employees' views of sources of information and management communications on 5 Shaft of Vaal Reefs West during this period (table 2.3).

Table 2.3 - Ranking of sources of information at 5 Shaft,
Vaal Reefs West, 1987

Pre-strike		Post-strike	
Role	%	Role	%
Union meeting	74	Public address system	84
Co-worker	60	Written brief	82
Written brief	57	Co-worker	75
Public address system	38	Union meeting	70

Before the strike the only source of information regarded as important by more than 70% of the men was the union mass meeting. After the strike, the union mass meeting was still considered to be important, but two sources associated with management had become even more important: response to the written brief distributed by management rose from 57% to 82% and response to the public address system increased from 38% before the strike to an incredible 84% after the strike. Such a dramatic shift in attendance to management media indicated that the managers on 5 Shaft had really got some- thing right in their communication with employees.

Exactly what this was came to light when we asked the men why management communication on the shaft had been so effective. The following quote is a telling example of a trend we discovered: one man said it had been effective because management "used the PA system and the written briefs to say something. During the strike a certain Mr. Botha was using the PA system to beg us to go back to work". The fact that the man could name Johan Botha was of paramount importance.

Johan Botha was assigned the job of managing the shaft in 1986, after a particularly gruesome series of events. There had been a union-organised execution of four team leaders from the shaft. They were brought before a large group of singing hostel residents, made to stand on wooden tables and stabbed to death with broken charge sticks. Unfortunately, because all four were Sothos, a massive con- flagration ensued between Sothos and Xhosas because the Sothos were not going to stand by idly while their countrymen were being slaughtered by Xhosas. In the course of these events Johan Botha was appointed to manage this shaft. By that time all operations on the shaft had ceased because the workers were busy butchering each other at the hostel.

Botha addressed the problem by entering the hostel all by himself, without weapons or security support. Armed only with a megaphone, he walked into the centre of the fray and appealed to his men to stop killing each other. This was how he introduced himself to his men.

Subsequently Johan Botha repeatedly demonstrated this very real, human concern for his people as the head of an operation where people's problems were actually attended to. He set the scene for the remarkable response of his employees during the 1987 wage review strike which took place about 18 months after the fights of 1986.

On the first day of the 1987 wage review strike the 5 000 men who worked on 5 Shaft did not report for duty. Along with the rest of the e 44 000 employees on Vaal Reefs they went on strike. On the second day of the strike Johan Botha went to the hostel and over the public address system the appealed to his men to return to work. His plea met with an astonishing response: but for a few hundred "bit- tereinders" his men heeded his call and returned to work.

These events had two important implications. First, Botha's men returned to work, despite the fact that his message was exceedingly contentious. One must bear in mind that this was the second day of the biggest single wage strike in South African history. All the other shafts on Vaal Reefs remained on strike while the men on 5 Shaft went back to work. In other words, the men on 5 Shaft accepted a message of immensely questionable content because it came form Johan Botha. Secondly, not only did the men attend to the content of the mes- sage, but from then on they listened to the public address system. This was not because it was such an exceptional medium - on the contrary. Technically it was poor (it buzzed and distorted) and, in addition it suffered from the same problem of transience as the video. The reason the workers paid attention to this medium was because of the man who was using it: Johan Botha.

In other words, both content and medium gained credibility because they were associated with a man who had credibility. After all, in so far as the issue of content is an ethical one (since it is principally concerned with truth), it also raises the key issue of the truthfulness of the speaker. In simple terms: if I trust you I will believe what you are telling me. This trust is not gained through mere speech. The speaker must act in such a way as to convince his listeners that he is sincerely interested in them and not just concerned with what he can get from them.

Management communication is therefore concerned with three issues, each of which contains the other like the layers of an onion. On the periphery we find the issue of least importance, i.e. the medium. You can get any medium to work for you, even the video.

Inside the medium we find a more fundamental concern, namely the issue of content - what is being said here? Remember that content is an ethical category because it concerns truth. What is being said is assessed in terms of whether it is true or not.

Inside the medium we find a more fundamental concern, namely the issue of content - what is being said here? Remember that content is an ethical category because it concerns truth. What is being said here is assessed in terms of whether it is true or not.

Within the content resides the most fundamental concern with regard to management communication, i.e. the credibility of the source. Who are you to be saying these things? If I trust you I will believe and accept what you have to say. On the other hand, if I do not trust you I will be suspicious of whatever you tell me - even if it is the truth. After all, as we saw from the example of management who briefed their employees on their pending retrenchment, truth can be used very successfully to terrorise people.

We can therefore conclude that all the expensive communication inventions the world has to offer will not be of any use to a man- ager if he is not regarded as trustworthy. On the other hand, he will be successful in his communication - irrespective of what he says or how he says it - if, like Johan Botha, he is regarded as a genuine and caring leader who looks after his people. The essence of successful management communication is therefore the same element as that which renders leadership substantive. It is by actively pursuing the well-being of his subordinate that a leader earns loyalty, trust and a willingness on the part of the employee to listen to and obey him. No amount of talking, however flowery or eloquently expressed, will achieve the same results. In fact, if the employee knows from experi- ence that no one is concerned with him or his problems, this kind of rhetoric may only serve to make him cynical.

This perspective also serves as a comment on the provision of information by management. Volker Hooyberg believes that a caring manager will make it his business to keep his people informed of aspects that affect them. While this is obviously true, it may well obscure the fundamental issue, which concerns the intentions of the manager. Let us take as an example the question of whether employ- ees should be briefed regularly on the financial performance of the company. I know of two mines that subscribed to this policy.

The interesting fact about these operations was that they were both marginal. This leads one to suspect that the managers were briefing their employees in order to focus their attention on the weak financial situation of the company. An employee who is alerted to the fact that the company, and therefore his job, is on unstable ground is less likely to engage in disruptive behaviour. What is therefore presented as a generous and empowering provision of information is actually a control mechanism used to invoke fear.

The acid test as to whether a manager is prepared to provide financial information for the right reason, is whether he will be prepared to brief employees when the operation is highly profitable. It is astonish- ing how few managers are prepared to do this. I recall a particularly acrimonious interaction between Volker Hooyberg and a manager at Vaal Reefs West (who is by no means a poor leader) with regard to this very issue. "It is fine to give people financial information if the mine is marginal," this manager said, "However, here on the West Division we are making a profit."

Management Visibility

A tenet of popular wisdom holds that good mangers communicate. Another one states that good managers are visible, they "walk" the operation, they are known and seen by the people. On the face of it, this second tenet makes absolute sense and therefore it is easily regarded as a magic wand that will cure all ills. This is very dangerous because a thorough review of the implications or significance of the manager's being "visible" may reveal potentially disastrous consequences.

We once did a survey on a West Rand mine where the climate of employee opinion was particularly poor (fig. 2.6). Management had attempted to improve the situation by introducing a structured management visibility programme whereby managers would routinely walk around the hostels just as the men were returning from shift. To our amazement we found that men who had actually seen a manager on his walkabout trusted management less than men who had not seen one! This discovery caused great consternation on the mine and also among us, since it was in direct contradiction with the view we held and the advice we were giving at the time.

On careful consideration, however, we realised that this finding was not at all as surprising as it initially appeared to be. Let us assume that at my workplace, my day-to-day experience of those in charge of me is that they are not interested in me at all, that they show no concern for my problems. In fact, the organisation I am working for is slowly devouring me.

Figure 2.6 - Trust in management on Mine L related to
management visibility

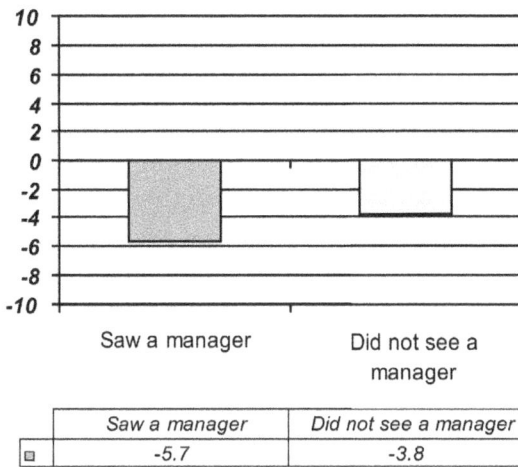

	Saw a manager	Did not see a manager
□	-5.7	-3.8

Suddenly one fine day, a man whom I am told is a very important manager arrives at my workplace with a magnanimous smile, asking people here and here for their names, and then departs. This exercise is repeated on the odd occasion while my daily experience - that my supervisors want as much as possible form me for as little as possible - remains unchanged. I am therefore confronted with a senior manager who is trying to present a caring face while my actual experience of my supervisors is that they do not care at all.

The real danger here is that by presenting himself to me, the senior manager comes to personify to me the organisation. In other words, I can now see with my own eyes the one who is responsible for it all, and he is smiling! Let us assume, then, that I experience the organisa- tion as evil, that I believe it is consuming me. It is only logical that I will come to regard this visible manager as the cynical incarnation of the evil I experience daily. Small wonder that I will trust him and his kind even less. Not only is he responsible for the fact that I am disadvantaged every single day; he even has the nerve to come and announce himself with a broad smile.

In fact, making the manager visible on an operation where people are not looked after may have disastrous consequences, particularly in contemporary South Africa. We once did some investigative work on a Free State mine where the senior manager was very visible. Every brief carried his picture. Photographs of him adorned virtually every wall and he frequently walked the hostels. However, trust in management was poor (fig. 2.7), since employees generally felt that their problems did not receive any attention.

One day, during one of his hostel walkabouts, this manager had to beat a hasty and rather undignified retreat from the hostel with a hoard of enraged, tyre wielding workers in hot pursuit. They wanted to kill him. The only thing achieved by making the manager visible in a poor trust situation is that the man's life is put at risk.

At this point it will be worth our while to reflect again on the example, quoted earlier, of Johan Botha's intervention in the Vaal Reefs 5 Shaft faction fight of 1986. He was new on the shaft at the time of the fight and nobody knew him. Yet when he made himself visible by his personal intervention in the fight, he was not killed. On the contrary, he re-established peace in a hostel at war.

The point is that his incredible courage was tangible evidence of his genuine concern for his men. He did not make himself visible for the sake of being visible. He made himself visible because he wanted his people to stop killing each other.

This shows that pursuing management visibility for its own sake amounts to confusing the essence - which is true concern - with the attribute - being visible. Obviously, the manager who looks after his people will be seen. However, the manager who does not look after his people cannot but be viewed with cynicism when he puts himself on display.

Disciplinary Procedures

In 1988 we were asked to do a climate survey on a shaft at a mine in the Orange Free State that had experienced a very severe series of conflicts. In 1986, four team leaders had been executed in the hostel by union members. These executions were very similar to those on Vaal Reefs 5 Shaft in that the men were made to stand on wooden tables and were then stabbed to death with broken charge sticks. Like the incident at Vaal Reefs the execution was carried out in the presence of the hostel residents who were sitting in the arena singing freedom songs. However, these killings differed from those at Vaal Reefs in one important respect: one of the team leaders who was exe cuted was a Xhosa, and the other three were Sothos. This served to defuse any possible confrontation between Sothos and Xhosas with regard to the executions.

A year later the union branch committee organised an attack on the shaft offices with the intention to replace the entire management team on the shaft with union members. In order to ensure that the attack would be successful, a *sangoma* from Transkei was summoned to give the attackers a special ritual scarification on their foreheads which would make the bullets turn to water. However, true to form, management had an *impimpi* (spy) in the branch committee and was therefore fully aware of the plan.

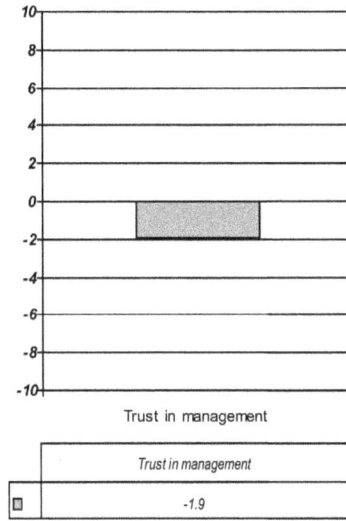

Figure 2.7 - Trust in management on Mine P, 1987

In fact, management's information was so accurate that they knew every detail of the impending attack. On a certain afternoon, the branch committee would approach the section manger in charge of the shaft and present him with an ultimatum to reinstate four employees who had been dismissed for a serious misdemeanour. When the manager refused (which they knew he would) they would mobilise the hostel residents to attack the shaft offices. The committee actually wanted an armed confrontation with mine security, since they were confident that the *sangoma's* scarification would make them invincible. Being fully informed of the time and nature of the planned attack, management also made preparations for war. The entire security contingent of the greater region was alerted and on standby, and all white employees were requested to vacate the shaft premises as quickly as possible after shift that afternoon. Only a handful of people were left by the time the branch committee arrived with their ultimatum. A little while later pandemonium erupted.

Numerous employees were shot in the confrontation, but what horrified senior management most was the macabre way in which two of their colleagues had been put to death. Inexplicably, the section engineer had returned to the shaft and entered the quadrangle of the shaft offices just as the battle commenced. He was later found savagely butchered on the veranda of the shaft office. The other man, a senior mine security officer, had his head literally split in two by a panga wielding unionist.

Senior management's reaction was probably the only appropriate one under the circumstances: they instructed that order had to be reinstated on the shaft at whatever cost. Consequently, the surviving members of the union branch committee ended up behind bars, the union was de-recognised, and the branch committee offices were shut down. Supervisors and overseers on the shaft were instructed not to tolerate any lack of discipline whatsoever, and were also assured of management's full support in re-establishing discipline on the shaft.

This strategy worked. Sabotage on the shaft stopped, and within weeks production reached levels unknown for years. Management felt that employees were generally very happy with the changes. All intimidation in the hostel had ceased, and bizarre murders (like a man being killed quietly while having supper by someone sticking a bicycle spoke through his spleen) became a thing of the past.

The only thing that worried these managers was that they did not have any concrete information on employee opinion. They felt that employees felt a lot better about them than they did in the past, but they did not have any means to test this view because the mechanism by means of which employee opinion was gauged in the past, i.e. the committees and the union, were no longer operating. It was therefore to assist management in obtaining this information that we got involved in surveying the climate of employee opinion on the shaft.

Management found that results of our survey depressing. We discovered that, despite the events of '86 and '87, trust in the union was still high (fig. 2.8). Trust in management, however, was poor. In fact, our final diagnostic statement could only be described as a woeful affair, and the managers concerned indicated that they were keen to have these poor results explained. There was a bit of information contained in the survey which could do just that.

One of the questions we asked the men was whether they had personally experienced any problems in the course of the last six months. The most common problem mentioned by interviewees who said they had experienced a problem was that they had been unfairly treated in a disciplinary matter (table 2.4).

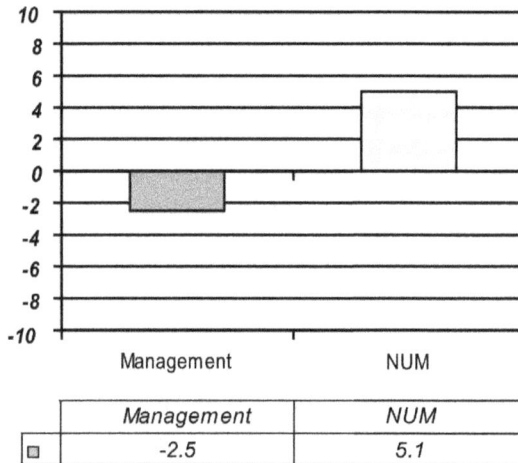

	Management	NUM
□	-2.5	5.1

Figure 2.8 - Trust in management and NUM on Mine Q in 1988

Table 2.4 - Problems experienced by employees on Mine Q in
the six months preceding the survey

Problem	Frequency
Unfairly treated in a disciplinary action	12
Not permitted to go home to attend to a family problem	9
Promotions blocked	5

Some of the examples given by these employees were indeed evidence of unjustifiably draconian disciplinary action. One man said that he had been sent to an underground store to fetch something on his second day underground. When he arrived at the store he found it closed and, not knowing what he should do, waited for the store to open. A passing shift boss found him there and immediately charged him with loitering. In the ensuing case, the man was found guilty and given a final warning.

These claims reminded of a very interesting conversation I had underground with a mine overseer who was introduced to me as Oom Gert. Oom Gert was an old man and he had been in the industry for many years. He was one of those people whose life-tempered wisdom could keep you enthralled for days. In our discussion the issue of discipline was raised. "In the old days," Oom Gert said, "if I had a problem with a 'boy', I took him down a centre gully, and then hit him with a pipe until he wet his pants!" He laughed, but as soon as he saw that he had obviously offended my liberal sensibilities he looked embarrassed and fell into a fretful silence. After a while he continued: "But today," he said, "today I can no longer do that. But now," and at this point he beamed, "now we have a disciplinary code."

Oom Gert had therefore made a mental connection between beating people until they wet themselves and applying the disciplinary code. But, disciplinary codes are generally instituted to protect people from the arbitrary abuse of authority. In this case, however, the code was used to pursue the arbitrary abuse of authority.

People were being charged at random for the most insignificant actions and maximum penalties were then imposed - all as a result of strict adherence to due procedure. This accounted for the fact that management had lost credibility to the union despite the fact that, from a certain point of view, their crackdown on the union had turned the workforce into a captive audience.

Management's handling of the whole issue of discipline had done them more harm than good, especially in that it did not subscribe to the core value of all disciplinary action: it was not seen to be fair. Moreover, this discipline, as Oom Gert had demonstrated, was affected in terms of the very disciplinary code that was supposed to ensure fairness.

This example demonstrates that fairness cannot be trapped in a code. Ultimately, the most sugary words in the world can be used to beat people until they wet themselves. Fairness is a human quality, it lives in the hearts of men and women. In other words, it is fair leaders who will discipline fairly. Relying on a procedure to ensure fairness shifts the emphasis from the necessary moral quality that a man of power needs to exercise command, to a surrogate and essentially artificial collection of procedural niceties that would seek to render the morality of the leader irrelevant.

The really disturbing thing about surrogates is that they assume the guise of legitimacy by being put forward as values. Thus, rather than being a convenient set of rules used to circumscribe the arena in which substantive fairness is established, procedural fairness becomes an end in itself. In other words, fairness has shifted from being a concern with a fitting retribution for an infraction, to being the proper adherence to the conventions that prove that the infraction has taken place.

This is equally true for the legal apparatus of modern society. Justice is seen to have been done when a man who is guilty as sin, gets away with it on the basis of a technicality. Fairness is also regarded to be associated with proper access to the technicians of the system, i.e. lawyers. It therefore follows that the accused's chances of acquittal are in direct proportion to the quality of technical expertise he can afford to buy.

Many aspects of our society are based on this theme. We have, for example, the modern value called democracy. However, on careful scrutiny democracy is revealed not to be a value at all, but a systemic factor. After all, the core value with regard to governance is that it should be just and protect those in its charge. Kings can be just, as well as lords, generals, presidents or prime ministers. The systemic arrangements through which they attain their exalted positions have precious little to do with whether they subscribe, in their day-to-day exercising of authority, to the deeply human concern that men of power must be just and care for those in their charge.

We see than that the notion of the surrogate slices deeply and mercilessly into the world as it is presently understood and structured. It lays bare the motive behind putting forward a surrogate, in so far as it demonstrates that the surrogate is always a sham or artificial attempt to deal with discontent so that an essentially illegitimate state of affairs may be perpetuated.

The basic rule of how the surrogate functions amounts to an elevation of the trivia of form to the status of excellence. The real danger here is that this exercise eventually makes people cynical of the essence itself. For example, let us assume that an employee has witnessed five disciplinary interactions that were correct in terms of the code but, at the same time, utterly and obviously unfair. One would have empathy with him if he exclaimed: "Ha! Fairness! There is no such bloody thing. There is only expediency."

We begin to see, therefore the serious consequences of employing a social science graduate (in our frame of reference, a mere mechanic) to deal with the social and human ills that are a direct consequence of a cosmology that has banished and trivialised the human spirit. The whole exercise only serves to entrench the disease.

The Union

The statement is frequently made that management's job is to produce, and the union's job is to look after people. In commenting on this idea I would like to refer to the job we did on Vaal Reefs West before and after the 1987 wage review strike. The reason for this is that the shift in employee opinion that took place during the strike with regard to both management and the union has very important implications for the role of the union in an operation.

There was a noticeable difference in the way in which employees viewed the union before and after the strike. Prior to the strike the men cited the following reasons for joining trade unions:

- The union attends to employees' grievances (raised 32 times).
- The union is a spokesman, in that it represents employees (raised 12 times).
- The union negotiates for better wages (raised 12 times).
- The union protects employees from unfair dismissal (raised 10 times).
- The union protects employees from unfair treatment (raised 10 times).

I was surprised to find that the most important reason given for joining unions was attendance to grievances, since had not found this to be the case in any other industrial relations survey I had conducted. It came as even more of a surprise that employees regarded attendance to grievances as central to their assessment of management. Attendance to grievances is the criterion in terms of which management's role is defined and management earns the right to command.

Prior to the strike the union was also assessed in these terms, and was thus regarded as a rival form of industrial leadership. This dilemma about who the real leadership was, was indicated by this comment from an employee interviewed before the strike: "The union attends to all workers' grievances, especially work-related grievances because the mine ignores workers' grievances that it should attend to."

What this man was actually saying was that the reason why men were following the union rather than management was that the union was doing the things that management should have been doing.

The union had therefore earned the right to manage and exercise power, whereas management had not.

After the strike, the emphasis shifted from the union's attending to grievances to their representing employees to management who then, by implication, attended to grievances. This was reflected in the following responses:

- The union represents employees, i.e. it is a spokesman (raised 37 times).
- The union protects men from unfair treatment (raised 36 times).
- The union protects men from fair dismissal (raised 31 times).
- The union resolves grievances (raised 21 times).
- The union negotiates for better wages (raised 21 times).

Clearly, the union's attendance to grievances in the post-strike setting was of far less importance than it had been before the strike, with the result that the intercessory facets of the union's role became dominant. At the same time management was considered capable of attending to grievances presented to them by the union. This is shown by the following statement: "Workers wanted management to attend to their grievances because the union has a certain influence over management."

Before the strike the union had definitely been viewed as a contender for leadership. After the strike it had come to be regarded as an intercessor. The fact that the union was allowed to fulfill only this role implied that management was once again seen as the real holder of power on the mine.

It must be noted that it took three weeks of incredibly costly conflict for management to reassert its authority, to wrest the attention of employees from the union. The question remained, however, how long management would be able to hold the employee's attention. Most relationships of power commence with a moment of imposition, but imposition in itself does not legitimise the relationship. It merely creates a captive audience to which management then has to prove its credentials by doing the things that power is supposed to do.

Just as employees' view of the union changed during the strike, so did their view of management. We have seen that the fundamental criteria in terms of which management is judged, concern management's perceived interest in employee welfare. However, important changes occurred during the strike in regard to the ways in which motivated their view that management was either interested in their well-being or not. Before the strike the men who felt that management had an interest in their welfare motivated their responses as follows:

- Management attends to grievances (raised 15 times).
- Management provides work (raised 8 times).

Although attendance to grievances is obviously the crucial issue, the subsidiary reason of providing work is important in that it constitutes a positive appraisal of the basic nature of the relationship between employer and employee. This emphasis changed after the strike as evidenced by the following reasons which were then cited as proof of management's interest in employee welfare:

- Management attends to grievances (raised 29 times).
- Management provides sport facilities (raised 10 times).
- Management provides accommodation (raised 7 times).
- Management provides entertainment facilities (raised 7 times).

Apart from attendance to grievances, the other reasons given were concerned with some of the fringe benefits enjoyed by employees on the mine. In other words, the basic nature of the relationship between employer and employee was no longer an issue of concern, but rather the facilities that were made available to employees within the relationship.

We found a similar shift of emphasis among employees who felt
that management was not interested in their welfare. Before the strike, this view was motivated as follows:

- Management does attend to grievances (raised 19 times).
- Wages are poor (raised 15 times).

The subsidiary reason cited before the strike as proof that management did not care about employees' welfare concerned poor wages. Wages are associated with the basic contract between employer and employee, which means that these men were being critical of this basic contract.

After the strike there was a shift in this emphasis, too, as evidenced by the following statements:

- Management does not attend to grievances (raised 18 times).
- Management discriminates against blacks (raised 16 times).
- Unfair dismissals occur (raised 9 times).
- There are not opportunities for promotions (raised 9 times).

Here the subsidiary reasons indicated a concern with job security and black advancement. These issues reflect a critical view of the place of the black employee within the enterprise, rather than of the basic contract between employee and enterprise. We therefore see that there was a shift in emphasis in both groups of employees, those who had a positive view and those who had been negative. Before the strike the fundamental nature of the enterprise had either been defended or criticised. After the strike it was the place of the black employee within the enterprise that was being evaluated, while the basic nature of the relationship between employer and employee no longer was an issue of concern.

It is hardly surprising that the basics of the establishment were at issue before the strike, since the union was still active at the time, promoting its leadership and making promises about bringing about a socialist South Africa. After the strike, employees were less interested in the establishment of this Brave New World than in finding their place in the sun in the present one. The parameters of the present establishment had, by implication, been accepted.

This suggests that employees were no longer looking towards the union to provide an alternative industrial leadership, but rather to represent them with management which, by implication, was once again seen as the legitimate leadership.

Employees no longer expected the union to effect a fundamental redistribution of wealth and power. They were looking to management to give them a sense of advancement and achievement within the present establishment.

This shift has several very important implications. First, it is suicide for management to allow a union to look after employees so that managers can be free to attend to production. When this happens, management is creating the conditions that empower the union to run the operation. Looking after people and attending to their problems earn one the right to command, which is why management should jealously guard these functions.

This does not mean that I advocate union bashing. On the contrary, the degree to which the union manages to sell an anti-establishment agenda to employees serves as an accurate barometer of the kind of leadership exercised by management.

This has positive implications for the way in which managers appraise the developing industrial relations scenario in South Africa. Many managers experience the rise in union activity and union militancy as frightening and paralysing. However, we have established that a union's bid for power can only be as strong as the degree to which management has capitulated with regard to providing leadership. The reins, therefore, are securely in the hands of the manager. However, the focus is not to take the union on, but to provide that kind of (proper) leadership that employees are trying to get from the union because management is not giving it.

Finally, one cannot but comment on the mentality that favours invoking a structure to regulate the relationship between employer and employee so that employee discontent may be addressed. In the gold mining industry in the 1980's, for instance, we witnessed highly ritualised and stylised annual battles between the champions of the two sides: Cyril Ramaphosa and Johan Liebenberg. How this theatre could ever substantively address the problem of the legitimacy of the establishment remains to be seen. In fact, it constituted a massive diversion form the real focus of the problem.

In the final analysis it would appear that we were sold a monstrous smokescreen which would not and could not address the issue of legitimacy. This demonstrates a salient attribute of the surrogate: by its very nature it is a smokescreen, a decoy that diverts the attention from the real issue of legitimacy. The dialectic it sets up is hollow, without substance. Regardless of which side of the fence you are standing on, ultimately you are still singing in the chorus of control.

The Problem of the Surrogate

We often use the bullfight as a metaphor for the relationship between employer and employee. This is not altogether inappropriate, particularly in contemporary South Africa, where this relationship may be quite as macabre as the bullfight.

The first idea evoked by this image is conflict. In the industrial arena we see very real, sometimes fatal conflict between employer and employee. At this stage of our argument we have to reflect on why this is so.

This conflict exists primarily because of our assumptions about the relationship between employer and employee. If you were to ask managers why they think the people who work for them should do as they are told, most of them would say it is because they are paid to do so. In other words, we categorise this as a trading relationship that is contracted in the marketplace and concerns the buying and selling of labour. The employee enters the market with his alienable, saleable commodity called labour, and the employer with his money. They haggle about the value of the commodity, an agreement is reached and they embark upon the relationship with each party striving to maximise his own benefit. Both parties are taking, but neither party is giving and therefore conflict is born.

The next thing we learn from the bullfight metaphor is how the "matador", the manager, is presently dealing with his enraged opponent. He employs his "cape" (the personnel function), or some fancy footwork (such as management communications). These aids become a representation of the manager, but one without substance. They are decoys, essentially aimed at fooling the opposition, and they are exclusively concerned with control. They are used to render impotent the justifiable rage of the bull. The surrogate can therefore never address the problem of employee discontent. Rather, it seeks to contain, manipulate and redirect that discontent in such a way that it poses no fundamental threat to the existing arrangement.

This game, however is dangerous. As we saw above, each new surrogate ingredient that is added to the cauldron contains and simultaneously exacerbates the problem of discontent. It becomes yet another red rag to the bull. It does not take a genius to conclude that sooner or later this brew will explode. Returning to our metaphor, it is evident that there must be at least one loser. (Often there are two). The bull never survives the fight and frequently, neither does the matador.

This metaphor holds disturbing implications for the workplace. A workplace is successful if it produces a surplus (profit). A surplus itself has very interesting implications. Let us assume that three men, Peter, Fred and Vusi, work at a bakery where they bake a cake. Once the cake is cooked, it is cut into four slices and each of the three men gets to take one slice home. That leaves the forth slice, the surplus.

The existence of a surplus implies that the team of men produced something "bigger" than that which each of them took for himself, i.e. they gave more than they took. This means that surpluses are created by generous people who give more than they take. At present, however, it is commonly believed that the workplace, and indeed the economy, function because of the self interest of people, people who are trying to maximise the benefit they gain from one another, people who are taking as much as possible while giving as little as possible. This is obviously not true. People who try to take as much as they possibly can do not make the world go round, they kill it. What we have set up on the basis of these assumptions is not a workplace that will produce a surplus, but mutual cannibalism, people who are devouring each other. This is the case because the current worldview is creating people who think it is legitimate to pursue their self interest above all else, to take more than they can give.

In the course of our research we discovered the key to unlock the door and set us free from this impasse. We have identified the conditions under which employees will be giving - instead of taking - in their day-to-day work. These conditions will induce employees to do what managers want most of all: when instructed to do something by a manager, the employee will carry out the instruction willingly because he will accept that the manager has the right to tell him what to do, to exercise power over him. However, these are very special conditions, in that they are created when the manager actually gives to the employee.

I am not here referring to a giving of "goodies", but to giving concern and attention from day to day. If I know that the man in charge of me is really and truly interested in my well-being, that he gives of his time to attend to my problems and concerns, I shall gladly give to him whatever he asks of me and more. I shall not want to get away with as much as possible, I shall want to please him.

The real shift that has to occur for this kind of relationship between employer and employee to materialise concerns the fundamental nature of the relationship: it must be viewed as being based on power as opposed to being a contractual agreement. What ultimately takes place in the workplace from day to day is the exercising of power. Instructions are given and are either obeyed or undermined. There is no perpetual re-evaluation of conditions of service. In the final analysis, labour cannot be bought and is not alienable from the labourer. If labour is to be carried out, the labourer has to accept the command of those in charge of the workplace. At issue here is not the selling of a commodity, but the legitimacy of a relationship of power.

To get a perspective on this idea of legitimacy, one must draw a clear distinction between power and control. Power is that intangible something that becomes legitimate only when the person who is asked to "deliver" is willing to give of his best to the person in power. This implies that the one who is asked to deliver must want to please the person in power out of loyalty and love. This loyalty and love will result when the subordinate realises that his superordinate genuinely cares for him as a person. Control refers to all the measures imposed on a person in order to squeeze effort out of him in cases where legitimate power does not exist.

What I find really shocking about current leadership language is its managerial idiom: people are not led, they are managed. The implications are important, because people, as well as things, organisations and processes can be "managed". In other words, people are reduced to the level of inanimate things and processes; they are your resource, you employ them and you use them. The feel of the idiom is one of pulling levers and pushing buttons, of manipulating things to achieve your ends.

However, as far as people are concerned, there are only two kinds of "levers" you can pull - sticks or carrots. You can either seduce them into compliance or intimidate them into obedience. In both instances you will be appealing to the very worst in human nature: greed and fear, instead of appealing to that which is noble, aspects such as courage and generosity. In short, you will be appealing to the characteristics that cause people to want to take instead of those that make people want to give.

From this point of view managers destroy people because they reduce them to the rank of things, to bundles of metabolising tissue that take in what they need and excrete functional behaviour and waste products. Leaders, on the other hand, elevate their people, and make them realise that they are infinitely more than objects; they unleash the spirit of their people.

In conclusion, let us recap the salient principles:

• Employing specialist functions to deal with employee dis- content frequently constitutes decoy attempts at defusing the potential for conflict in the workplace. However, peace will not be maintained in the industrial arena until the managerial exer- cise of power has been legitimised. Legitimacy is achieved when leaders demonstrate an authentic commitment to protecting and furthering the interests of employees. This commitment is put to test whenever management is approached with a problem or grievance.

• Legitimate industrial leadership concerns the right to exercise power. The employee's primary experience of the exercising of power is associated with the routine issuing of instructions by supervisors. Therefore, command itself achieves legitimacy to the extent that the supervisor adequately represents the line of command's ability to give employees a sense of security and advancement.

• It is therefore vitally important for the line of command to function as a team that embodies this leadership ethic at every level.

Chapter 4

ESTABLISHING LEGITIMACY

On the basis of our experience with organisations such as Safripol, it is possible to posit a strategic human resources framework aimed at establishing legitimacy in an overall sense – that is, unless someone has the decency to put us to the stake for referring to people as *human resources*! Because the very words we use are so powerful, it is advisable to clear out some terminology before going any further.

When I talk of a "framework", I am referring to an (inanimate) skeleton to which (living) tissue is attached. In other words, a frame- work provides the context or form for content. Of the two (form and content), content is the essential and fundamental issue. So, the point of establishing a framework is to provide an appropriate context for whatever content one wants to further. Before constructing a frame- work it is therefore essential to understand exactly to what use that framework will be put.

Bearing all this in mind, we can now list our concerns in taking on the challenge of establishing legitimacy within an organisation:

* Content
* Strategic framework
* Change intervention (the process of change)

Content

Although we have already viewed the issue of content from various angles, it would be useful here to review the essence of our approach to the human being, both in terms of the general approach of management and in terms of what that approach should be. In other words, let us establish, clearly, the content of the discourse relating to the person in the workplace.

Figure 4.1 - The three types of people found in the workplace

Three types of people are found in the workplace. In South Africa we refer to them as Baas, Koos and Klaas (fig. 4.1). Baas – who usually has an English surname – is the manager, i.e. the person responsible to the board for bottom line. Koos is the overseer, the one who – for the last eight decades – has ensured that the water was drawn and the wood was hewn. Klaas is the one who hews the wood and draws the water. Finally, one should not forget the wood and the water. The interesting thing about the wood and the water is that, regardless of whether wood or water or even gold is involved, the ultimate aim is to make money, to increase figures and numbers.

Now, if one were to ask Baas what his job was, he would reply, in all earnestness, that his job, i.e. that aspect for which he is answerable to the board, is the bottom line, the figures. In fact, his job is to make the figures. To do this, he goes to the marketplace and he buys himself X units of labour, kilojoules, schooled in the way that "Kose" are schooled, and Y units of kilojoules schooled in the way that "Klase" are schooled. Back at the workplace, he pours the appropriate amounts of kilojoules into the correct buckets of an organigram. To this he adds a dash of plant and a pinch of supplies. He then kick-starts the lot and the machine starts spitting out figures.

> *Because people are used, they feel that management is taking from them and therefore they want to take as well. The framework currently used in management is producing people who are in it for the taking.*

While this approach makes tremendous sense to the intellect, it is disaster in terms of the heart because both the Kose and Klase in the organisation are being told that they are Baas's kilojoules, the human resource he uses to get his figures. Now, if anybody were to tell you quite unashamedly that you were his resource, that you were at his disposal, you would certainly feel most unhappy. After all, nobody likes to feel used and most people recognise that there is something obscene about using people.

And so the inevitable consequence of managing human resources is that the people concerned get discontented because they feel used. This is a problem, because they are also the ones who are actually producing the figures. Consequently the process of producing the figures becomes more and more of a crisis as the "human resources" become less and less willing to make their contribution.

This will remain unchanged unless those in charge of the workplace recognize that what is at issue is not a fair price for a bag of kilojoules, but the legitimacy of a relationship of power.

You cannot sell your capacity to work. You cannot put your kilojoules in a box for other people to plug into their organisation. If you work for someone you have to do what they ask of you, i.e. you have to submit to their exercise of power. What is at issue between employer and employee is not the price of a commodity called labour, but the legitimacy of a relationship of power.

We have argued that a relationship of power gains legitimacy only when the superordinate honestly cares about his subordinate and does not use him.

In other words, power is legitimate and acceptable only when the powerful are not in the game to use or get something from the subordinate, but to give him.

If we were to reduce this perspective to a number of axioms, the first one will undoubtedly state that:

Axiom 1

> *What is at issue between employer and employee is not the price of a commodity called labour, but the legitimacy of a relationship of power.*

This statement needs to be clarified and to do this it may be appropriate to consider the issue of power in the light of parenting.

Parenting is the very first relationship of power to which the human being is submitted, and as such it could reveal some of the core issues in the questions surrounding power.

The first thing that springs to mind about a parenting relationship is that the two parties are of different sizes; one party – the parent – is big, and the other – the child – is small. The big person's job with regard to the small one is quite specific, namely to create the conditions under which the small person may grow and become big. So, the function of the powerful is to enable the powerless. Where the powerful do this, their power is legitimate, i.e. it is doing its job. However, where the aim of a relationship of power is not to empower the subordinate that power is illegitimate. If a parent's upbringing yields adults who are essentially still children we know that parent has failed.

The illegitimacy of the current management framework is borne out by the fact that the human being is diminished at the outset by being described as a resource. Clearly, the aim of the relationship as it is at present is not for the powerful to give anything to the sub- ordinate, but for the superordinate to accumulate while using the subordinate as a means to that end. Such a relationship contains an element of the perverse. The parent who uses his children for self- gratification is clearly at odds with the correct order of things. We can now formulate the second axiom:

Axiom 2

> *A relationship of power is legitimate only if the aim of that relationship is the empowerment of the subordinate party in the relationship.*

This suggests that the task of the powerful is to give, and not to pursue the maximisation of their benefit at the expense of the underling. Of the two parties, the parent, the powerful one, is the one who gives, and the child is the weak one who takes.

This suggests that empowerment means moving from weakness to strength, which is the same as moving from taking to giving. This brings us to the third axiom:

Axiom 3

> *Empowerment means enabling the one who is weak, in need and therefore taking, to become strong and capable of giving.*

So the powerful are those who are not taking, but those who are generous with giving of themselves. Power is not to be confused with status or position. (In fact, the thirst for status is a terribly self-centred motive.) Empowerment therefore does not mean to elevate people to a higher level in the hierarchy, but to make generous human beings.

One may go further and argue that just as children grow into adults, and the mature or final product of childhood is adulthood, so the purpose of being human is to become powerful, or generous. The proper stature of the human being is therefore generosity, which leads us to the fourth axiom:

Axiom 4

> *The power status of the human being is that of servant.*

This axiom spells the end of technocracy, because technocracy is based entirely on the assumption that the proper human motive is self-interest. In technocratic terms economies and societies function because people are trying to get as much as possible from each other for as little as possible. Clearly, this is nonsense.

People who maximize their own benefit at the cost of another do not make the world go round, they kill it. You are not here to get anything, and the only inalienable right you have is death. In fact, death is the only thing of which you can be absolutely sure. Death is testimony to the fact that you are not here to get anything, but to give everything. The most predictable thing about your life is that you are going to lose it. Your task is not to accumulate, but to expend. You have not been created to take, You have been created to give.

A "people strategy" for an organisation (the term, human resources, is now *verboten*) would have to focus on enabling generous people. We can therefore argue that a successful company is one that enables people who are on this earth to give something, and not one that employs people who are here to get something. The beginning and end of our people strategy should be about understanding what people should be giving, and enabling them to do so.

Returning to our picture of Baas, Koos and Klaas, we can modify it to indicate what giving means for all three parties (fig. 4.2).

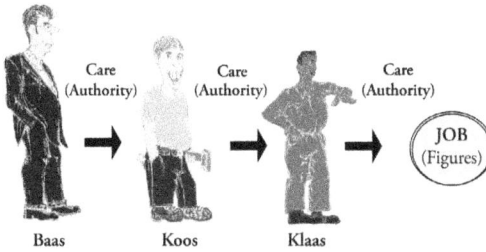

Figure 4.2 - A people strategy for Baas, Koos and Klaas

What Baas and Koos have to give to a subordinate is leadership. This means that they must be enabled to be true leaders. What Klaas gives is, in the first place, the job and, in the second place, its implications (the figures or bottom line). The work my colleagues and I have done over the last few years suggests that it is possible to affect a successful change intervention in an organisation on the basis of these perspectives.

Strategic Framework

A strategy aimed at enabling people to give would have to meet the following requirements:

1. To provide everybody in a leadership position with the authority and knowledge to care for and empower others.

The moment this statement has been made, it becomes necessary to ask oneself who is actually exercising power. It is not Baas who gives instructions, but Koos. So Koos has to understand that his job does not concern figures; his job is making noble and generous Klase. In other words, Koos has to care about Klaas. The point of his job should be Klaas himself, and not what he is getting from Klaas. Not only should Koos care for Klaas, he should also be given the means to care for him. In other words, Koos must be entrusted with real authority over the people who work for him. In practice this authority could include matters such as cash advances, leave, discipline, even hiring and firing.

Obviously, all Kose must be trained to enable them to handle and administer all aspects of the authority entrusted to them with regard to their subordinates.

However, if Koos has to drag his heart by its strings through the gate every morning because he feels his boss does not care about him and that he is just another number in the organisation, it is extremely unlikely that he will care for the people who work for him. The implication? The very thing that is at issue between Klaas and Koos is also at issue between Koos and Baas, i.e. the legitimacy of a relationship of power. This has a number of consequences:

First: If Koos's job is Klaas, Baas must understand that he is not allowed to interfere with Klaas. He may not, for example, give Klaas an instruction, or interfere with Koos while he is giving Klaas an instruction. Baas's job is to make Koos big, not to reduce him.

Second: Baas has as much work as he has direct subordinates. For example, if he has six people reporting to him and each of those six people has ten subordinates, Baas must understand that his job is to enable six leaders, not to manage sixty-six subordinates. Baas must care for Koos, and he must have the authority to do so.

This naturally holds true all the way up the hierarchy. A legitimate relationship of power between subordinate and superordinate needs to be established at every level of the organisation.

In addition, knowledge with regard to the implications of the four axioms should be transferred specifically to leaders, for example:

Axiom 1

- All the things normally regarded as the exclusive preserve of personnel departments must be returned to line function. Human resources people should only fulfill a consulting role.

- A wage only pays for the delivery of a body on site. It does not establish the right to expect work from that body.

- The leader is responsible for his subordinate, and not for production. The person who produces is responsible for production.

Axiom 2

- The leader's primary task is to grow people. He must therefore be given all the knowledge and skills required to be an effective teacher and coach.

- The leader should be assessed and rewarded in terms of the degree to which he has "grown" people through giving to them. The person whose job it is to produce should be assessed and rewarded on that basis, and the degree to which he has served (enriched).

Axiom 3

- The leader has to be taught specifically how to deal with employee discontent; this should not be the exclusive reserve

of industrial relations specialists. In so far as the discontented are takers, it is the leader's job to deal with them since leadership has to turn takers into givers.

- The current management dialectic and its implications (e.g. affirmative action and democratisation of the workplace) should be thoroughly re-examined from this point of view.

Axiom 4

• The leader needs to face and understand the fact that there is much more to life than merely manning a place on the organigram. He is existentially answerable for enabling others, which is a far more important than being answerable for a bottom line.

2. To provide everyone who is carrying out a task with the knowledge necessary to understand why he is doing it.

This means that a people strategy should be aimed at enabling all employees to understand that they are in the workplace to serve the client. The implications of service to the client amount to turnover. Employees should understand that to be in the workplace primarily to earn a wage is being there for the wrong reason.

Therefore a people strategy should be very clear in its purpose to endow employees with the nobility and meaning of the task in terms of its contribution to the well-being of others. This endowing, or handing over, has both a qualitative side (what people do with our products) and a quantitative side (how much money we earned, i.e. to what extent we were financially rewarded by our clients for the way in which we served them).

3. To provide everyone doing a job with the knowledge and skill needed excel at it.

In so far as a people strategy aims at making people who will serve by doing a task, it should include the implications of doing a task excellently, with virtuosity. Therefore, it should involve more than just a transfer of technique; there should also be a transfer of love of the task and honour of the trade.

The Change Intervention

Because of the change in our assumptions with regard to the relationship between employer and employee the implementation of a people strategy would have two major thrusts, a leadership thrust and an employee reporting thrust.

If the relationship between employer and employee is not to be viewed as a transaction for the sale of a commodity (labour), but as a relationship of power, then Baas's job entails elevating, ennobling and "growing" Koos, and Koos's job is to do the same for Klaas.

However, if elevating Koos is going to be Baas's primary concern it means that the current focus of his job – producing figures – has to shift. In the past, people used to be the means of producing figures, but now figures have become the means to elevate people.

The shift in focus in Baas's job means that the figures are entrusted to those who actually produce them, i.e. the Klase. The reason for entrusting Klaas with the figures is not just to have something to talk to him about. The reason is to entrust to Klaas the task or mission of the organisation.

In this manner the necessary context is provided to give Klaas the opportunity to participate creatively in the execution of the task and in any attempt at gain-sharing.

We have looked at the leadership thrust (which is aimed at legitimising relationships of command down the line) and the employee reporting thrust (which is concerned with entrusting the figures to Klaas) of the change intervention. Let us now determine what a change intervention that would address both these components would look like.

Leadership Intervention

The essence of an intervention seeking to legitimise relationships of command down the line would be to have a facilitator act as consultant to leaders in the organisation.

The consultant will have a two-fold task. First, he would have to present the key ideas on legitimacy to the senior team of the organisation in order to win their (even partial) support. Second, he would have to spend time with the team leader's subordinates, either singly or in a group, to determine whether the superordinate subscribes to the criteria he has endorsed. This discussion would centre around two questions: "Does your boss care about you?" and "Do you have the authority to do your job?"

The feedback from the discussions with subordinates would be relayed to the leader of the group by the facilitator in order to bring to the fore any discrepancies in the leader's behaviour with regard to the criteria of good leadership which he himself endorsed.

The entire process is of a very informal, *ad hoc* nature and the time needed to complete it at any level in the organisation will be determined by the problems identified at that level. However, there is one vitally important principle, namely that major issues identified at top level must be resolved before the process is taken further down the organisation.

The informal facilitation process described above may be changed to assume the more structured form of a formal change intervention. This involves two related processes, i.e. leadership training and trust or team building, which take place simultaneously or one shortly after the other.

There may be two reasons for preferring to conduct a formal intervention. First, a client frequently feels uncomfortable with a consultant who seeks to conduct an informal intervention because it does not have a definite cost or time limit. Second, although conducting a formal workshop is time consuming (people are taken from their work for a certain length of time), the intensity of exposure made possible by having a focused period of time to spend on the theme serves to entrench ideas.

Managers are put through a leadership workshop to give them the opportunity to carefully consider the consequences of the arguments we put forward. For example, if we say that the current technocratic world view is savage and non-human, it is vital for the manager to understand fully why this is said, and what the moral consequences of this statement are.

Therefore, a leadership course must create conditions under which the participant can clearly differentiate between power and control, between leading and managing. The distinction made should not be based on information alone. The process we use in our workshops exposes people to a number of instances of manipulation, so that they experience it first hand rather than merely "understanding" it. When we then say that it is inadmissible to treat people like manipulable things, all participants know exactly what we are talking about.

Once the ideas around legitimacy have been entrenched among a group of managers, it is possible to get that group to confront each other in terms of their new understanding. This can be done in a formal workshop which could include a number of elements, such as a structured discussion of the elements of trust, the key issue we have to deal with since the problem of control is essentially a problem of trust. The reason one controls people is that one does not trust them. The aim of the workshop is therefore to provide a structured opportunity for a group of managers to exchange feedback on their own leadership. It must be stressed that a leadership workshop can be conducted to good effect only once participants have been exposed to the essential criteria of leadership.

Based on our experience, a successful leadership intervention should include the following components:

•   Facilitation

•   Leadership workshop

•   Trust / team-building workshop.

Employee reporting (1)

(1): With regard to the topic of employee reporting I am deeply indebted to my brother Jerry. Any thoughts I have on this matter are really his; this section must be seen as a poor paraphrase of Jerry Schuitema's perspectives.

No process implemented to legitimise the establishment of an organisation would be complete if employees were not entrusted with a full review of the organisation's performance. It may be argued that employee reporting is the only authentic precursor to any attempt at empowering employees, whether by means of a participative management process or a gain-sharing scheme.

In so far as employee reporting means entrusting the figures to Klaas, some kind of sensitisation or training is required for the figures to make sense to Klaas. This training should include two major elements. The first is general economics and transaction, and the second is basic accounting. Training in these fields will enable Klase to understand the figures communicated to them.

Extreme care must be taken, however, not to entrench any of the alchemical perspectives of yesteryear during training. People are given figures so that they may gain insight into what they are doing and how they are contributing to the creation of wealth. By its very nature the approach of enabling subordinates is an ethical one. This means that the erroneous arguments which hold that economies thrive on the self-interest of people cannot form the basis for this kind of training.

The point of departure in training should be that all transaction is rooted in a moral principle, namely that the seller should be of authentic service to the buyer. Let us assume that you buy an apple from a shop on the corner. You take a big bite out of it – and find a decapitated worm wriggling at you. Obviously you are not satisfied with your purchase and you return it to the shop-keeper. If he reacts by yelling at you in some foreign tongue while chasing you out of his shop, you would (understandably) be most upset because he did not fulfil a basic rule that governs all transaction: sellers have to serve buyers. You would feel cheated and you would think that the shop-keeper serves one person only: himself.

To demonstrate this point further, let us assume that you have a broken lawn-mower. Luckily, two lawn-mower mechanics have recently put up shop on adjacent premises in your neighbourhood. You take the lawn-mower to the first mechanic who fixes it for a certain amount and also gives you a guarantee for his work. Two weeks later you are back to square one: the same thing has gone wrong with the lawn-mower and you take it back to the mechanic, indicating to him that you would like him to honour his guarantee. His response is to yell at you (in English this time) and chase you out of the shop. He refuses to honour his guarantee and says the machine broke through your mistake.

So you take the lawn-mower to the fellow next door, who charges you exactly the same price and gives you the same guarantee as the first mechanic. Two weeks later the same part breaks again, and you return the machine, demanding that he honour his guarantee. Let us assume that the second mechanic responds with genuine concern. He takes the machine back, apologises and promises to do his utmost to fix it. Although he spends additional time and money on it to make sure that it does not break again, he does not charge you for it because he feels that is part of his guarantee.

The question is, if your lawn-mower should break again next year, which of the two mechanics would you take it to, the first of the second? Obviously you would take it to the second man because you would have realised that the second fellow was as good as his word. When he saw you entering his shop he did not ask himself how he could get you to part with your money, but how he could help you, how he could be of service to you. Because you recognise that, you went back to him a second time and so you became to him that which is most valuable to the seller: a loyal customer.

These examples illustrate that economies become weak when people try to grab as much from each other while giving as little as possible. Economies are strong when people have things to offer, to give. This argument holds at both the macro- and micro-economic level. The reason for Japan's economic success after the devastation of World War II, for example, was that the Japanese were prepared to work for a bowl of rice a day. They gave a lot for very little and so they became world players despite having been virtually destroyed. The Americans, on the other hand, gave the world promissory notes (dollars) and accumulated as many goods and resources as they could lay their hands on. They took much and gave little. Consequently, the American economy is in a shambles.

The one theme that runs through all these examples is that economic strength is not based on what you accumulate, but on what you give, how well you serve. A sound economy has nothing to do with getting; it has everything to do with giving.

It is very important for employees to understand this principle, since this will create the correct atmosphere for communicating company results. Figures can ennoble people only if the people can relate to them as an indication of how they are doing, how well they are serving. Therefore, the view that all economies must be market driven and that sellers must serve the market and not just pursue their own self-interest creates the backdrop for a more detailed look at figures.

Probably the most effective way of introducing employees to figures is by explaining the value added statement to them. The value added statement is based on the following idea: an elderly lady goes to the flea market where she buys a ball of wool. She uses the wool to knit a jersey which she takes back to the flea market where she sells it. She paid R10 for the wool and gets R20 for the jersey. This means that she added value of R10 to the wool by her own effort.

This basic understanding of how figures work is as true for a large organisation as it is for the elderly lady. The proportions of a typical value added statement would also be very similar, although all the added value does not go to the equivalent of the elderly lady, that is the people who produced the goods. The reason for this is that large organisations have stakeholders, other than employees, who also have a claim to value added.

A typical value added statement could look as follows:

Turnover...100

Costs... 50

Value added... 50

Distributed as follows:

    Employees..................................... 30

    Reserves... 10

    Tax.. 6

    Dividends..................................... 4

The main reason for giving the figures to the employee in the form of a value added statement is that it provides a very simple framework for understanding the concept. Any new figures that are communicated, for example, would affirm the same basic principle and would therefore serve to entrench and widen the employee's basic understanding. This also provides the opportunity to examine and explain the role of each category in the statement. Such explanation could include the following points:

Turnover

The turnover of the organisation is the total amount of money that has been paid to it by clients as a reward for the service rendered to them by the organisation. It is the equivalent of the money the elderly lady was paid for her jersey.

Costs

The costs represent the total amount of money that has been paid to outside suppliers for materials and services rendered. Costs therefore represent those things that were used in the process of producing wealth. In developing this theme, it is always a good idea to examine what contributes to the costs of an organisation, in other words, what main supplies are used by the organisation.

Value added

Value added represents the difference between costs and turnover. It refers to the value of the human knowledge, time and effort that were added to external supplies to enable the organisation to offer the client that for which he was prepared to pay. Value added therefore represents the wealth that has been created by the organisation. This wealth is distributed among the following stakeholders: employees, reserves, tax and dividends.

- **Employees.** Employees are normally the principal beneficiaries of value added. In fact, in the average South African company employees receive around 60% of value added. This is an important fact in that it counteracts the view that the interests of the shareholder and those of the employee are separated by an enormous divide. Compared to the percentage size of wages, the dividend paid to the shareholder is very small. It is also important to account for the interests of employees and shareholders on the same side, so that the one is not regarded as existing at the expense of the other.

- **Reserves.** It is important for employees to understand that just like a farmer has to retain some seed (or at least the funds needed to buy it) to be able to sow again the next year, so the company has to keep some funds in reserve in order to replace or expand present production capacity. Reserves therefore represent the company's savings and are intended to enable the company to expand or to weather difficult conditions.

- **Tax.** While most of us bitterly resent the tax we have to pay to the Receiver of Revenue, it is only fair to indicate to employees that unless the Receiver gets his pound of flesh, no infrastructure will exist to get the goods from the plant to the client.

- **Dividends.** The dividend is the reward given to the shareholder for running the risk of financing the organisation, thereby enabling it to conduct business. From this point of view, dividends have a legitimate place since they represent a reward for a risk taken.

It is important to note that this sort of training serves no purpose if it is conducted in isolation. It merely lays the foundation for something much more important, which is the ability to communicate the financial performance of the company to employees on a routine basis.

The question now arises: "Who should handle the communication?" Referring back to our picture of Baas, Koos and Klaas it is clear that Koos should be imparting this information to Klaas, and not Baas or a communications surrogate. This implies that Koos must have more thorough understanding of the figures than Klaas because Koos must be able to defend the figures.

It is therefore important to train Koos extensively in terms of the ideas he has to communicate to Klaas. Koos must know, for example, that the financial success of post-World War II Japan can be ascribed to the fact that the Japanese were giving instead of taking.

The most important reason for both Koos and Baas to have this perspective is that it will change their attitude towards figures. The current understanding (which I have tested with a sneaky questionnaire) is that businesses exist to make a profit, which means that the manager sees his job as the bottom line, i.e. return on investment. This view has devastating implications. It means that the manager of a manufacturing concern sees all the souls who have to drag themselves through the gate in the morning, as well as the plant, materials and supplies as a huge still which has as its sole aim the distillation of a tiny droplet of blood called a dividend. This can only be described as barbaric! It reduces the whole exercise to an unedified grabbing in the interest of the smallest beneficiary of value added. (No wonder the employee sees his interest as being directly opposed to that of the shareholder.)

Proper reflection on the value added statement makes it abundantly clear that the trader should not exist simply to pursue the bottom line, which represents the rapacious interest of only one of the recipients of value added, namely the shareholder. He should see his role as being of service to the customer. In so far as turnover indicates the degree to which the market rewards a business for its service, it is the final measurement of whether the trader has been doing what he is supposed to do: has he and his employees been of service to their clients?

Providing the manager with this kind of understanding will also influence his ability to provide proper leadership. Without this under- standing the manager sees himself purely as representing shareholders' interest. In other words, he is no more than the shareholders' lackey and as such his sole purpose is to ensure that shareholders get their return on investment. This has to change.

If we argue that the most important objective of the manager is to enable the people who will go out and serve a market, turnover is certainly the most important measurement of the extent to which this has been achieved. It is only when the client has been served that value is added and wealth is created. Once wealth has been created it can be distributed, and the shareholder is only one party out of four who will receive a slice of the value added.

This puts return to the shareholder in its proper perspective. If the manager sees his job as enabling people to serve a market and ensuring that all parties who have a claim on value added receive an equitable reward for their contributions, wealth will be created to the benefit of all.

On the other hand, if the manager basically regards his job as keeping the shareholder satisfied, everything else will eventually suffer because the shareholder's interest will receive unbalanced emphasis. It is similar to one organ in the human body growing out of all proportion. Like cancer, such an undue emphasis will eventually destroy the entire body. Therefore, in the interests of all parties, the manager has to overthrow the shareholder as final arbiter of the purpose of the organisation and occupy the vacant throne himself. After all, he occupies a unique position at the centre of the organisation, and is therefore the only person in a position to take charge in ensuring the benefit of all concerned.

To return to the issue of a change intervention, we have indicated that the main reason for providing these perspectives to the manager is to put him in a position to communicate the financial performance of the organisation to the employee. This brings us to the final aspect of a change intervention, namely the actual communication of figures. We envisage a reasonably regular provision of financial information to employees, at least every quarter. Like any discussion on communication, there should be two aspects to this discourse, namely the essential matter of content and the issue of media. Let us deal with media first. While it is imperative that every immediate supervisor should handle most of the actual communication, consistency must be maintained with regard to facts and presentation. This can be achieved to a large extent by arming the supervisor with reference material beforehand. Such material can be quite simple and straight-forward like a poster-sized value added statement depicting the actual figures. If the need is felt to have something more elaborate, a video or slide presentation may be used.

However, the purpose of any media used must be to enable the supervisor to come across more convincingly. Media should in no way detract from the supervisor.

Regardless of the peripheral media, the main documentation must be simple and in print. It could, for example, consist of two pages, one featuring the figures and the second with space left open to note queries and questions. The latter point is important because the system by means of which information is cascaded down the organisational hierarchy must also allow for the upward communication of concerns and suggestions.

All the surveys I have conducted on communication indicate that people do not find a medium credible unless it allows for reasonably immediate interaction and feedback. In practice this means that any question the supervisor cannot answer immediately should be taken down in writing and given to the supervisor's boss for comment, after which the supervisor should clarify the issue with his subordinate. At every level of the organisation the manager concerned should collate all the feedback he got from his people and communicate this up the hierarchy. This would give senior management a feel for concerns being raised in the organisation that may require further communication.

Once this process is in place it commits employees to a vision with regard to the performance of the company, and also enables them to contribute towards improvements. In this manner a foundation is laid for authentic employee participation.

Let us now deal with the most important element in the communication of information to employees, i.e. the content. If the reporting of financial results assumes the form of a boring rendition of figures on a quarterly basis, chances are that the employee will lose interest. It is therefore crucial that the figures are interpreted beforehand in order to present them to the employee in as interesting a manner as possible.

Change provides an excellent opportunity for putting together a stimulating presentation. If, for example, a key supplier were to announce a sudden price increase it could serve as a focus point for discussion during the communication. This will not only promote understanding of the problems associated with sudden price increases, but will also serve to increase employees' understanding of the value added statement.

We have mentioned that employee reporting is the only proper precursor to employee participation and gain-sharing. It provides a basis for employee participation in that it informs the employee of the reason for making a contribution.

With regard to gain-sharing the possibilities are legion. Let us assume that after a process of sensitisation, all concerned (management, employees and shareholders) agree on the proportions of value added that each stakeholder should get, for example 60% to employees, 20% to reserves, 6% to tax and 4% to shareholders in the form of dividends. If the organisation doubled its value added in a given year, each stakeholder, including employees and shareholders, would get proportionally double the amount they got previously. The opposite is also true. If, because of adverse trading conditions, the organisation only succeeded to add half of the value that it added in a previous year, the benefit to each stakeholder would also be half of what it was the previous year.

This has an interesting implication. It refutes the view that an organisation is a collection of functions on an organigram, each of which has a market value. Rather, it suggests that an organisation is more like a group of people baking a cake. The bigger the cake, the bigger the slice everyone gets to take home. If, however, the cake should get smaller, it makes infinitely more sense for each stakeholder to get a thinner slice than to throw some people to the wolves (by cut- ting a few boxes from the organigram) so that the others can still get their bigger slice.

In fact, this is existentially correct. We know that if there is famine in the land then it is morally just for everybody to get a little less so that those who are not wealthy do not starve to death. This is not socialism, it is common sense. In medieval times it would have been unthinkable to evict some peasants from the estate so that the others could get the same amount of food they got the previous year. That would have been regarded as unjust and would probably have brought the king's wrath down on the lord. Today, however, people are retrenched when the bottom line on the balance sheet does not do what it is supposed to do. Ultimately, an organisation will grow and prosper if all the people associated with it share both in its good and bad fortune. But, this sharing should not happen out of some sense of gimmickry (e.g. share-participation schemes); it must reflect a situation where the task or mission of the organisation has been genuinely entrusted to the people who do the work.

This will mean that the leaders will have come to terms with the fact that it is not their job to produce a glowing balance sheet, but to enable people. The workers, on the other hand, will have realised that they are not employed to earn a wage, but to serve the client.

In both cases the people concerned must be human beings in the fullest sense of the word. They must be people who know that they exist to give something, not to get something. Every single transaction they engage in must be measured against the criterion of what the employee can contribute and how he can improve the situation. The question is not: "What is in it for me?", but rather: "How can I serve? How can I be of help?"

Chapter 5

THE THREE ATTENTIONS

Going back to our depiction of Baas, Koos and Klaas, it becomes clear that the essential requirement for a manager who wishes to change his focus from managing to leading is that instead of concentrating on the figures (or, what he can get from his people), he should focus on enabling his people.

Proper leadership is therefore about where you focus your attention, about what is important to you. In this regard we can distinguish three ways of dealing with people at work – and, by implication, with others. We shall refer to these three ways of looking at others as the "three attentions".

The *first attention* is the attention of the manager who views people as resources that he applies as means or tools in the production of figures. In other words, when he looks at his people, the only thing that interests him is what he can get out of them.

The *second attention* is a refined version of the first attention, because it is based on the manager's awareness that if his people where to catch on that he is interested only in what he can get out of them, they will become discontented and revolt. He therefore has to dress up his taking as giving, which means that he gives in order to create the conditions where he will get. From a certain point of view these waters are even more dangerous to navigate than those of the first attention because they involve authenticity. People are generally more comfortable with someone who brazenly pursues his self-interest than someone who does this under the pretense of pursuing some noble cause. This is, in fact, the very issue surrounding surrogacy.

Although the second attention is dangerous, it is an essential articulation point between the first and third attention precisely because it is the battlefield of the struggle for authenticity, which is at the core of the third attention.

The *third attention* is the attention of the leader who genuinely strives to make his people big, to transform them into giants. In other words, he is not there to get anything from them, but to give them something.

To understand leadership one has to understand these three attentions and their implications, because shifting from the first to the thirds attention requires a personal revolution which does not affect only the leader in the work situation. Because the central issue of the third attention is authenticity, this attention is not merely a behavioural mask worn to work along with a suit. It demands a transformation at the very core of your being, and to achieve it, you have to turn your life upside down. Shifting from the first to the third attention will affect your approach to every facet of life because it requires a constant attempt to rise to serving the other, instead of remaining inert and getting the other to serve the self.

The First Attention: I Am Here To Get

This is the attention of the person who acts purely on the basis of his immediate self interest and whose sole concern is with what he can get. Therefore, it is the attention of the *immature self* who regards the other to be there only to serve it.

It is infantile to think that the world is there to serve you. This attitude amounts to believing that when you are hungry all you need to do is open your mouth and yell for someone else to come and feed you. Not only is this childish, it is also ignorant.

We have discovered that bigness is about generosity, and now we also find that being correct, for the adult, is about generosity. So, while you are selfish you are not only childish, you are also wrong. You are not doing with your adulthood what you should be doing. You are in a state of loss and you are missing the point. The first attention is therefore the attention of self in darkness, the self that has missed its purpose.

In as much as the first attention is about being here to get, it is also about accumulation. In other words, I derive my significance from the things I have accumulated. I am significant because I own.

I base my sense of worth on my achievements – not only in terms of things I have acquired, but also with regard to biographical detail. Any person who thinks that he is important because of what he has achieved thinks like a child. Associated with the belief that achievement is all important, is the idea of arrival, of "getting there". This mentality leads the person to believe that as he gets older he becomes more significant because the mass of accumulations associated with him becomes bigger and bigger. Every step he takes forward is about getting more. He wants to have more both in terms of position and biographical trivia because it makes him secure.

The belief that achievement brings security is evidenced by what we may call the Irish Sweepstakes Syndrome. People suffering from this syndrome believe that at some stage or another they will make it so big that they will never have to work again. It is about arriving, in style, forever. This is a selfish, childish illusion. Nobody marries the prince and lives happily ever after, because five years after the wedding the prince discovers that he is gay and breaks the princess' heart. So, to our utter horror we discover that even those who have arrived, the rich, are in deep, deep trouble and thoroughly discontented with their lot.

Arrival is about perpetuating the status of the child. When I arrive, when my ship comes in, I am going to lie on a faraway beach, surrounded by nubile maidens popping grapes into my mouth. I will have nothing to do but bask in the sun and metabolise. Arrival is therefore synonymous with remaining static, not with having to act. I will remain in this blissfully static state and the world will serve me. Ah....Paradise!

So, once you have arrived, you can rest and be lazy. Action is not important, change is not important. Arriving is important, staying the same is important. The essential characteristic of a person in the first attention is that he thinks in terms of problems and solutions. In other words, what confronts him is a static state called a problem and he has to do something to it in order to arrive at the solution, which is also a static state. His doing or acting is merely a brief interlude of change and discomfort between two (blissfully) static states. In terms of this attention, problems and solutions are basically about staying the same, about exchanging one static state for another, one stillness for another.

Another way of putting this is that what surrounds me is wrong because it is not doing what I want it to, it is not serving me. So I am going to put it right so that it will do what it should, which is to serve me. My doing is the inconvenience in the middle which I will have to put up with to get it to serve me. I do this in order to achieve that. I do not do this in order to do this. What is interesting to me is not what I give or do, it is what I get.

Thinking strictly in terms of problems and solutions is the same as accounting for the world by a means of a set of functional cause and effect relationships. Cause is a static thing and effect is a static thing and change is the uninteresting and insignificant thing that separates them.

The person who attempts to connect the world in a pattern of casual or functional relationships is actually bringing the world to a halt and disjointing it in a series of measurable leaps that impact on each other in a stop-start way. In fact, the very act of measuring something causes all movement to cease. By measuring you com- pare something to an accountable record, you freeze the measured moment. What is lost in the moment is the flow of life itself, which does not stop and start, but moves and changes continuously. Existence as we know it is not characterized by stillness and security, but by movement and change.

This brings to the fore a very important point about functional thinking, namely it is an attribute of the first attention. Functional thinking means moving from stasis to stasis, because both cause and effect are static.

The ability to deal with chains of cause and effect is the key thinking skill of technology. You cannot manage a system unless you are familiar with the impact one part of it has on another part of it. This is in fact implied by the very term technology which refers to the rule of those who are skilled in technique, in other words, the rule of those who know how to manipulate various measurable factors in unison in order to achieve a predetermined result. These people know what they want and they know how to get the world to give them what they want. Remember, the world is there to serve them and they apply their knowledge of casual relationships to get it to deliver.

Ultimately, technocracy is a world view of use, which is exactly what the first attention is about. Something is interesting only because it is useful, because you can get something from it. It is only logical then that any discourse in the first attention will focus on how to do something, which is a technical concern, rather than why things should be done, which is a moral concern. We could therefore say that technocracy functions properly only in the hands of people who function at a level of the first attention. Technocracy requires a smallness and a meanness of spirit to work.

When berating technocracy for running affairs at a level of the first attention, you must realise that this is not happening out there, in some irrelevant by-water. It is being done to you, your world is being run at the level of the first attention. This is evidenced by the credit economy.

At present society functions on the basis of the principle buy now, pay later. Another way of putting this would be to say take now, give later, or you can take without having to give, which means that you assume the status of a child. Indebtedness means being weak and small because it means that you have taken without having given.

Not only individuals have been indebted, but entire nations have been indebted by governments. This is true not only in the case of so-called capitalist states, but throughout the world. Our age has witnessed a massive diminishment of stature of the human being despite an avalanche of rhetoric around human rights. The price of technocracy has been our humanity, regardless of whether you are clinging to a television-inspired fantasy of living in the most advanced age known to man.

A final point to be made with regard to the first attention has to do with the issue of work. The major principle concerning the nature of work in the first attention is related to the view that the other is there to serve the self. In other words, the world is a resource for the self to use for its own purposes. However, by its very nature, a resource is expendable, once you start using it, it gets depleted. Therefore, the consequence of living in a world where your affairs are being run on the basis of the first attention is that the world is dying. It is being used up.

Another truth about work in the first attention is that it is only done in order to achieve something. Working for the love of the task, to be giving something, is inconceivable within this framework. In fact, work in the first attention is based on the shocking discovery that opening your mouth and yelling do not suffice – you do not always get what you want simply by doing that. Sometimes you have to do something, you have to work, to get what you want. In other words you have to give something to get something. At this point the first attention slips into the second attention because it is the point at which you decide that the world is not good enough because it is not making you happy, and so you will have to fix it.

The Second Attention: I Have To Give To Get

In so far as the second attention is about giving to get, it is the penitential attention. For example, I run in order to get thin. I expend the energy of running in order to achieve the state of slenderness, which means that I am giving to get. I am not running for the sake of running. In fact, the activity itself is entirely insignificant in that it is merely a means of achieving the desired state of slenderness. Therefore, running is the hard work, the suffering I have to endure, in order to get to what I want to have: a slim and handsome Mr. Myself. This means that I regard running as a punishment.

The moment an activity is embarked upon to get something else, the activity itself turns into punishment. What is true of the second attention, therefore, is that it is the adolescent attention, or the attention of the self in conflict.

Anyone functioning at the level of the second attention is negotiating with life. His attitude to the other is one of "If I do this, if I give this, I want that result or that reward". In terms of relationships with other people it amounts to a constant haggle to achieve equilibrium, to a contractual relationship signifying that "I will make you a little big if you make me a little big". The other is granted significance to the extent that the self is granted significance by the other.

The basic attitude of a person functioning at the level of the first attention is that the other is less than the self, that the other exists to serve the self. A person of the second attention indicates to the other that he will give what the other wants if the other reciprocates equally. In other words, the second attention person views the other as equal to the self. However, because this equality is basically modeled on haggling, it is indicative not only of a self in conflict, but of an entire social nexus in conflict – a social nexus peopled by individuals who are exerting pressure on each other to give what is wanted, with the threat of withholding what the other requires if the goods are not delivered.

From this point of view much of what is generally regarded as being liberal democratic thought can actually be typified as second attention thinking. Liberal thinking assumes everybody to be equal, in other words everybody has an equal right to get. However, commensurate with this point of view there is the realisation that different people will want different things and that at least some of these are bound to be incompatible. The function of authority in society is therefore to provide a framework of control to manage conflicts of interest as and when they arise. In other words, the purpose of power is not to elevate the powerless, but to maintain equality and – by implication – mediocrity.

Thus the liberal framework does not challenge the assumption that people are here to get and this has highly significant consequences. If we assume that humans are essentially motivated by self-interest rather than generosity, we must recognise that, all things being equal, the overriding sentiment in society will prove to be a threat to the very fabric of society. In other words, if left unchecked, people will all be taking more than they give thereby wreaking havoc in society. The focus of the liberal discourse is therefore not one of taking on this selfish motive, but of finding the most equitable way to structure and control the implications of selfishness. Further to this, the issue of legitimacy then becomes a structural and systemic one, i.e. one that would seek to establish an ideal framework for society or, in other words, a "system that works". Taken to the extreme, this becomes grand Utopian thinking: the things that have to be done for society to arrive, to get there. There really is something extremely adolescent about this approach.

One can therefore say that the current political dialectic, broadly scripted between the Right and the Left, is the equivalent of first and second attention thinking. On the Right one basically has first attention thinking because of the insistence on a strong central authority with the capacity to keep a tight reign on all the selfish individuals who are out to destroy society. By contrast, the Left is horrified at the arrogance of such an authoritarian approach because it violates the golden calf called equality. Everybody has an equal right to get and heaven forbid that anyone should interfere with someone else's equal ity. The thoroughly convincing framework created by this dialectic traps us into assuming either the Left or the Right side of the coin as the position we are prepared to defend to the bitter end. The real tragedy is that Left and Right are sides of the same coin of selfishness, because both perspectives are based on the point of view that man's highest motive is greed. The current political dialectic is therefore devoid of substance in that it cannot account for a society that has as its aim the enabling of generous people who are here to give.

We have said that a person in the first attention says: "I am here to get", a person in the second attention says: "I have to give to get" and someone in the third attention says: "I am here to give". Relating the three attentions to a metaphor of light and darkness, one could say that the first attention is darkness, the third attention is light and the second attention is greyness. Progressing from darkness to light, there is a point in the middle where the greyness changes from being mainly dark to being mainly light. In other words, at the centre of the second attention there is an articulation point where a view of predominant getting changes into a view of predominant giving. This is the point where the conflict shifts from discontentment with the world to dis- contentment with the self. One could refer to this point as the birth of conscience.

We have indicated that the second attention is the attention of the self in conflict, the penitential attention. It also represents an essentially discontented view, and it starts off, initially, as discontentment with the world. The sentiment is one of: "I have done all these things to arrive, to get there, yet I still have not arrived. It's just not fair". However, at some stage or another the logic of this dilemma must begin to suggest that I may have been doing the wrong things, i.e. the fault might possibly not lie out there, but with me. The reason why I have not arrived is not because there is anything wrong out there, but because there is something wrong with me: I am not good enough, I am guilty.

In this manner the focal point shifts from what I am getting to what I am doing or giving. This establishes the ground where I pay attention to what I am doing. At the same time I am confronted by the distinction between doing to do, which is authentic, and doing to get, which is false. The test for authenticity therefore lies in my reason for doing something. If I engage a challenge that requires me to give to something that is greater than my self-interest, I have passed the test of authenticity. The second attention is therefore the terrain where the battle for authenticity or sincerity is fought. Its entrance is self-interest and its exit is the courageous engagement of the noble struggle.

The Third Attention: I Am Here To Give

The third attention is distinguished from the other two by the view that the other is not here to serve the self, but that the self is to serve the other. The first two attentions are conditions of weakness (and therefore immaturity) because if you need to get something from other people their capacity to withhold that which you want puts you at their mercy. On the other hand, if you are here to give something their withholding whatever they want to is quite irrelevant. Strength is therefore based on what you offer and weakness is based on what you get.

The person of the third attention is capable of giving because he has befriended his death and has accepted it as his advisor. This means that he has come to terms with the inevitability of death and the fact that he cannot take anything he has accumulated with him. He therefore knows that he is not here to get, but that he is here to give, because the most certain thing about his life is that he is going to die and lose everything. Therefore he knows that the correct way to view life is that it is about giving it all.

The third attention consequently involves living in the light of the fact that one is here to expended. This can be taken even further in that one could say that only the things that exist are the things that are expended. The embryo that stays locked in its shell forever remains nothing but a potential bird. It is only once the potential for being a bird is expended, i.e. used, that the embryo becomes that which it was designed to be.

In human terms this means that your potential to be what you were created to be can never be realised on the basis of that which you accumulate, but only on the basis of what you expend. Life is there- fore not about what you accumulate because it is not about what you get, but about what you give. In the first attention you think that you are arriving and that you will eventually arrive. Operating in the third attention means knowing that you are not arriving, but that you are departing. There is no security, there is no static state to be achieved because you are rushing toward irrevocable and utter transformation. You are not here to stay the same or to arrive. You are here to change, the most elevated statement of which is death itself.

Whereas the moment of getting is the moment of arriving and therefore of becoming inert, the moment of giving is the moment of acting and therefore the moment of movement or change. Growth implies change. To become bigger means to leave smallness behind. Acting on the basis of what you want therefore means staying the same, whereas acting on the basis of what you can contribute, how you can serve, means that you create the conditions necessary for you to rise beyond yourself.

The danger of functioning in the third attention is to misconstrue giving as a grand, millenarian gesture of giving everything immediately. This belief is actually the second attention in disguise, because the assumption is that you will arrive the moment you give everything you have to give. For a sapling to become a tree takes time, it cannot happen instantaneously. Each moment of growth means that motion is maintained by taking the next step. The tree grows by increment, not instantaneously.

Giving in the third attention therefore means giving that which is appropriate or required at that specific moment. You do not engage in a cattle killing. To take the next step you have to confront only the moment facing you and give what is required. Every moment presents you with two possibilities. The one is to ask yourself what is in it for you, what you want and can get. The other is to ask yourself what can you give, how can you contribute. By responding in terms of the second option you release the potential of what you can be, what you were meant to be and so you are delivered into the next moment transformed, bigger than you were before.

An essential requirement of this way of being is that you affirm the moment. It is the status of the man who does not wish to be in the shade when he is in the sun, and does not wish to be in the sun when he is in the shade. In other words, it is irrelevant whether that which surrounds you also suits you. You need not fix your surroundings to correspond with your expectations. What is relevant is that you engage your surroundings and give that which is appropriate. "The other" for you is whatever surrounds you at a specific moment. Trust the totality of the other so that your good auspices are unleashed.

There is nothing you can do to ensure that you get what will be beneficial to you. What is of benefit to you will be granted to you. You cannot define that which is done to you, that which you will receive. You can only define what you do. This means that you have to assess the situation to the best (noblest) of your knowledge and act accordingly. To do this from one moment to the next will make you greater from one moment to the next. This is what it means to realise your potential as a human being in the same way that a sapling grows into a tree. The third attention is therefore the attention of the mature self, the self that is accomplishing its purpose.

Acting to the best and noblest of your knowledge in the third attention means to act with courage, generosity and care. Acting courageously means acting in a way that is contrary to the fear of death. Acting with generously means in a way that is contrary to the fear of poverty. Acting with care means acting in the light of the fact that significance lies with the other. In other words, everything that surrounds you right now forms part of the other and it is not a mistake.

On the contrary, it is particularly significant to you because you are standing at the centre. So, be fastidious in dealing with it, take care not to waste it.

Looking at the implications of the third attention with regard to people, you realise, first of all, that others are not here to serve you, but that you are here to serve them. However, your giving has to be appropriate in that it should affirm the other. This means that will you recognize the potential greatness of the people around you and that you will serve (or give) in such a way that this potential greatness may be realised. This perspective is extremely important because it shows that serving people does not mean being servile; it means doing the things required to make the other great and not the things that you think will elevate the self.

From one point of view this also means not tolerating mediocrity. Serving the other does not mean to allow him equality with the worst in himself, but to create the circumstances where he will rise to the best in himself, in other words, where he will start acting with generosity, courage and care. Serving the other is hard and difficult; it has nothing of the pink sweetness of candy floss.

If you were to compare the average chief executive with a man like Shaka in terms of the third attention in order to determine who is the barbarian and who the civilized man, Shaka would clearly be revealed to be the civilised man. Why? Because the essence of Shaka's project was to enable noble, courageous men who would be willing to give their all in battle. Furthermore, he could only enable others to have those qualities because he himself served as an example. He demonstrated, time and again, the true meaning of courage on the battlefield. At the other end of the spectrum, the chief executive has as his project the bottom line on the balance sheet and he uses however many people he needs as a resource to achieve the desired results. Instead of giving to them, thereby making them big, he is taking from them, thereby keeping them small and greedy.

You are big to the extent that you are serving, i.e. doing what a mature person should be doing. Serving is best described as acting in a manner commensurate with the intention to enable the greatness of the other. This means that you become big on the grounds of having made the other big. Your bigness is associated with his bigness. You gain significance because you made the other significant, not because you made him small or allowed him to remain lazy. This makes bitter commentary on the competitive spirit underlying technocracy. In the current situation the only people of significance are those who have won. In other words, in a technocracy you are significant only if you can demonstrate others to be less significant that you. However, in reality your significance is not based on the significance you take from others, but on the significance you give to others. The more you adhere to this principle, the more powerful you become, the more truly great you become.

Understanding significance is the same as acting with care. This kind of behaviour means that you do not regard the people you meet or your interaction with them as insignificant. On the contrary, you go to great lengths to ensure that you give to others exactly what they need to grow in their particular situation. By taking care to establish the significance of those around you, you elevate not only them, but also yourself. Therefore, the more you establish the significance of those around you, the more significant you become, and the more significant you become, the more care you will take to ensure the significance of others. By implication you cannot allow yourself even one moment of laxity since every encounter with the other should receive the best you have to offer.

To illustrate this, I would like to tell you about a man I have met. He manages a large furnace for foundry and has a few hundred people working for him. Four levels of management separate him from the people actually operating the furnace, which means that, in a formal sense, he is a very significant man.

In the course of a discussion I once had with him, he indicated that he was terribly frustrated with his subordinates. The reason for his frustration was that any casual remark he would make while walking around the furnace – even if he was merely thinking aloud

– would immediately be construed as an instruction by those two levels down the hierarchy. As soon as he had left these people would implement or execute what they thought had been an instruction from him. What really irked him was that because he did not have a thorough technical understanding of the working of the furnace, many of his so-called instructions had a very negative impact on production.

Because he was seen as significant whatever he said was regarded as serious and important. He could not afford himself the luxury of a frivolous remark. He could not afford to waste a moment because the implications of his wasting a moment were far more serious than for an employee further down the hierarchy. This clearly shows that being big is not synonymous with having arrived and being able to relax. Being big means greater responsibility and more astuteness. The greatest people are those who work themselves to a state of utter depletion and exhaustion, those who expend themselves and not those who preserve themselves.

Viewed from this angle, working or executing a task in the third attention, also acquires a special connotation. In the first and second attentions work is regarded as the activity engaged in by the self to get the other to serve it. In other words, it is about changing the other to suit the self. However, in the third attention the purpose of work is to transform the self through service to the other. This may sound strange, but I can explain by quoting an example.

While doing fieldwork at Hoechst's Trevira Plant in Cape Town, I had a discussion with a production foreman called Muhammad Moesavel. Eventually we got to the topic of how to teach people the intricacies of manufacturing fibre. This is what he had to say:

> *A manager comes in here to teach me or my crew to make fibre, and he brings with him a recipe book. He then points to the hopper at the top of the building and says: "You see that hopper up there? Well, this recipe says you have to put five tons of poly pellets in that hopper. Now, do you see that thermostat there? This recipe requires you to put that thermostat at this setting. And you see that tensioner? Well, you must set like this...." And in this way this manager will now talk us through 500 metres of production line of Trevira Fibre, step by step by step.*

> *He is a bloody mad man! This is not how you make fibre! If you want to make fibre the first thing that you have to remember is that you are not there to tell that fibre: "Now you be like this or like that." You must know that you don't do anything to that fibre. That fibre is going to be what that fibre is going to be, and my job is to help that fibre become what it will become.*

There are a number of implications to these words of Moesavel. First, he showed an attitude of service with regard to doing the job, which affirmed that which he was doing. In other words, he was not making the fibre. The potential fibre was already in existence; he merely helped it to be born.

This reminds me of the famous words of Henry Moore: "When I sculpt a horse I take away all the rock that doesn't look like a horse." In other words, Henry Moore does not create the horse; the horse is already there, in the rock. What Moore does is to serve the horse by taking away or cleaning up the excess rock obscuring it. From this point of view, cleaning or sweeping is the purest form of work or activity. It expresses what all work is or should be, namely to bring forth tidiness from chaos. For this to happen you must affirm that the tidiness is already in existence, thereby granting significance to that which confronts you. The next step is to serve that significance by picking up the broom and sweeping away everything that obscures it from view. In the process you are serving the significance of and elevating the other, which is precisely what elevates you in turn. So, work in the third attention is the activity that serves the other and thereby transforms the self. This is known as virtuosity.

Virtuosity therefore refers to doing a job correctly for the love of it – a point of view that is usually regarded as stemming from Oriental philosophy. In fact, it is a truly European idea because it was precisely to further the honour of the trade that the various guilds were established in European society. If you consider the actual skills needed to be a cabinet maker, for example, you will discover that you would need about two years to master them. Yet it took as many as ten years for an apprentice to qualify as a craftsman, not because that is how long it took to learn the trade, but because that is how long it took for the master to transfer to the apprentice the essential element, namely love of the task and honour of the trade. This transfer is not the same as transferring information from a book. As we have seen in the case of the foreman at the Trevira Plant, it is a direct transmission, from heart to heart, of what an attitude of service means in that particular discipline.

This brings us to the second major element implicit in Moesavel's statement, and that is how the job is understood. When the manager looks at fibre he sees a set of measurable quantities that can be transcribed as a recipe in a book. When Moesavel looks at fibre he sees something beautiful that he is going to serve so that it can see the light of day. The manager is fascinated by the figures and statistics around the fibre; Moesavel's fascination lies with the beauty of the fibre. To the manager, the world is a piece of functional machinery that can be divided into an almost infinite number of different units. Moesavel regards the world as a live entity in perpetual motion with a total meaning and significance greater than that of the sum of its various components. Therefore, an essential difference between the first two attentions and the third attention is that in terms of the first two, the world is reduced to numbers, whereas in the third attention the world is viewed as having a qualitative significance. The key to unraveling the consequences of the third attention is therefore to approach the world as having a qualitative significance.

The Key To The Third Attention

There are two poles to being, namely the outward (or objective) pole and the inward (or subjective) pole. These are synonymous with the observer and the observed.

Inward	Outward
(The observer)	(That which is observed)

Figure 5.1 - The two poles of being

You are an observer and, with regard to you, everything else (i.e. outside you) is that which you observe. In fact, you are encapsulated, surrounded on all sides by the observed, which means that you cannot escape it. The observed forms a sphere around you and you form its centre. You are not peripheral, you are not living marginally and meaninglessly on the edge. The fact that you are capable of observation, i.e. the fact that you are a conscious, sentient human being, puts you right at the centre of it all. You are the core, the turning point, the hub of meaning.

Once you have grasped this you realise that nothing that faces you or that happens to you is meaningless. The understanding that you are the focal point because you stand in the middle affirms the meaning of everything else because everything else stands in relationship to the middle. So that which is outside, surrounding you, is not arbitrary. It is not a random set of meaningless accidents. The whole grand canvass of being that surrounds you is not only unique to you because you alone stand where you stand. Its focal point is you. You are its observer and its affirmation or negation lies in no other hands than your own.

Two points of criticism can be leveled at the practice of surrendering your life to the machine. First, you are abdicating your meaningful position, thereby making your life peripheral. The current reign of the machine is perpetuated only because you acquiescence. You allow yourself to become the replaceable, to feel (and become) peripheral. Since only you can make your life meaningful this is a crucial point in that it implies that you are as responsible for the death of the world (its loss of meaning) as everyone else. By letting go of your birthright to infuse that which surrounds you with meaning, you are shirking your responsibility with regard to the immediate implication of how your surroundings actually function. The fact that the observed always surrounds the observer is not fantasy, it is real. This means that you have to let go of the responsibility and consequence of this tangible truth for an unreal, fantastic notion that you are peripheral.

Second, your meaning is stolen by those who are meaningless. The reason why people wish to be at the centre of a pyramid is that they feel being in this position somehow makes them meaningful. What they are actually saying is that by reducing others to meaninglessness they gain consequence. So the manager at the top of the cake or the gladiator on television assumes meaning because you are peripheral to him, and this makes him feel tremendously important, he does not understand that his own consciousness makes him significant in his own right. He needs to have his existence confirmed in some concrete way – which he achieves at your expense.

In a way both the theft of someone else's meaning and the surrender of your own are fearful responses to the actual status of things. From the point of view of qualities, the relationship between the out- ward and the inward being as we have described them have a number of consequences.

First, understanding that you are completely encapsulated by the outward being immediately creates you in a sense of being in awe. The mere knowledge that the outward stretches to infinity in every direction away from you and that you are inescapably locked in at the centre of its embrace, makes you feel that the outward being is grand, vast and majestic and that, by comparison, you are indescribably small. It is like looking down from the top of a mountain and looking around you and being dumbstruck at the grandeur of what surrounds you. Your central position therefore makes it possible for you to recognise the true nature of the outward being, i.e. majesty. At the same time and to the same degree you are silenced and in awe.

Just as this insight that you are standing at the centre of being may prove elevating, it is also terrifying. In the face of the immeasurable vastness of the outward you, you are utterly vulnerable. You cannot escape the outward, it is permanent and it can – and will – crush the life out of you sooner or later. This is a direct consequence of the qualities of inwardness and outwardness.

It is the nature of the majestic to ravish the beautiful, just as it is the nature of vastness to consume smallness. In the same way the observer, in so far as he is a minute point in an infinite sea of outwardness, will inevitably be swamped and annihilated. This is in accordance with the design of things, this is how things were intended to be.

In the wake of this insight, the outward no longer presents itself as majestic, but as monstrous, and the awe of the silence is replaced by a primal scream of unadulterated horror. So the realisation that you are the centre is revealed as a two-sided sword. You now have two options. You can either assume that the universe is indeed a friendly place, that there is a sense of design to it and that there is a fundamental purpose to things, or you can choose to suffer from clinically defined paranoia on the basis of your belief that the whole world is out to get you. In the terms of the evidence, both of these views are equally true. Choosing between them is a matter of belief.

In fact, from one point of view, the second option seems more plausible because we know that we are going to die. The first point of view, on the other hand, cannot be demonstrated; it has to be accepted in naïve good faith. It is faith alone that enables us to choose between sanity and madness.

What the savage world view has achieved, in a sense, is a life description that makes this critical confrontation irrelevant. If you are peripheral you can neither be terrified nor in awe because you are an irrelevant nothing.

Still, you must bear in mind that you have no say in choosing your position. Your being at the centre is a given, which means that believing yourself to be peripheral is pure fantasy. If you should accept the primary consequence of being at the centre as madness, it is evident that terror lies at the heart of this peripheral way of being. However, the consequences of this terror are softened so that some semblance of normality may be pursued.

From this point of view the savage world view perpetuates the lie that the human being is functional in making things so that he may be busy and therefore be distracted from the central existential issue which confronts him: death. In a sense, however, being saddled with the discomfort of your inevitable death makes it possible to see that there must be more to life, that there must be purpose. On this basis the inward moves out to affirm the world in an authentic and unconditional sense. Therefore, the good news is that although the outward looms over you in a terrifying way, you are at the centre, which means that you decide whether there is a purpose to life or not. If you are at the centre of the surrounding universe, it follows that your affirmation of meaning is the source of all meaning, just as your fear that it is arbitrary and ill-disposed towards you is the source of all fear.

These qualities of the inward and the outward have various attributes which are interrelated in much the same way as the qualities. In many esoteric traditions, a key symbol for the outward is the sun and the corresponding symbol for the inward is the moon. The sun is seen to be radiant and powerful, whereas the role of the moon is to reflect the light of the sun. In the same way the outward is powerful, it radiates. In fact, you are being bombarded with impulses from every conceivable direction.

The outward is radiating towards you every moment of the day and night. Your role (or duty) with regard to that radiance is to reflect it, to allow it to suffuse you. If you do not submit to it, you will not be able to fulfill your role of the awe-struck observer.

	Inward (The observer)	Outward (That which is observed)
Quality	Awe	Majesty
Attribute	Submission	Power
Symbol	Moon	Sun

Figure 5.2 - The inward and outward: their qualities, attributes and symbols

As shown in figure 5.2 the ideal attribute of inwardness is sub- mission, which means letting the outwards in, being a fascinated, awe-struck, child-like explorer.

The ideal attribute of outwardness, on the other hand, is power. The currently prevailing view of the self tries to equate selfhood and inwardness with biography. This is actually a terrible trap to fall into because a biography can, by its very nature, be objectified. As soon as the observer tries to look at himself, i.e. to turn himself into an object that he can observe, the inward is reduced to the status of the outward. The moon has to face the sun in order to fulfill its role of reflecting it. If the moon should try to look at itself or to reflect itself, it will no longer do what it was supposed to do and that is reflect the radiance of the sun. In fact, if the moon were no longer to face the sun and thus reflect its radiance, it would reflect darkness, the essential quality of both ignorance and perversity. Your eyes have been made to look at the other, to find the other fascinating. Should you try to look at yourself, i.e. to turn eyes inward, you would be extremely ugly.

Associated with this perversity is an inversion of the attributes of the inward and the outward. The current cosmology typifies man as the uninvolved, external manager or manipulator who regards the rest of being, the outward, as a resource for consumption. The inward man is the powerful one who imposes; the outward is that which is submitted, it is a resource. The result of this train of thought is that human beings live in the illusion that the rest of creation is here to serve them and that their acquisitiveness and selfishness form the single criterion for distinguishing between what is meaningful and valuable and what is devoid of meaning and value.

Not only is this view incorrect, but it also violates the balance between the inward and the outward. The human being is not here to gain, but to give and to serve. For as long as the human being maintains this humble and submissive attitude he is actually right at the centre of the universe, and he can celebrate living at the station to which he was called, which is being at the centre! However, this can be sustained only if the essential attitude of the person involves service and humility.

The discussion above suggests that there are certain moral qualities or ethics associated with inwardness and outwardness. Returning to the sun as a symbol for outwardness one is struck by the sense of radiance, warmth and beneficence emanating from the symbol. In other words, the outward radiates, it is generous. The light, sound and sensation bombarding you from all directions are a gift to you.

Seen differently, you could say that the table in front of you is not X units of wood, but that it is generous. The fact that you see the table means that it radiates its nature, it gives of itself, it comes to you. It spills out of itself and bridges the divide from where it is to where you are.

On the other hand, the generosity of the table has, from one point of view, not actually materialised until you let it. If the moon does not face sun the reflection does not happen. So to play your role as a seer, as the one who apprehends, you have to let the table in. If you close your eyes, or look at yourself or look away, you would not seethat which is around you and you would therefore not be able to give expression to your essential quality of being awe-struck. To truly see – and thus be human – you must want to see, you must be appreciative of the outward.

The moral element associated with an appreciative demeanour is gratitude.

It is the grateful human being who is of service to the rest of creation and therefore actually stands at the centre where he becomes the pinnacle of creation. We can therefore develop our pattern still further (see fig. 5.3).

	Inward (The observer)	Outward (That which is observed)
Quality	Awe	Majesty
Attribute	Submission	Power
Symbol	Moon	Sun
Ethics	Gratitude	Generosity

Figure 5.3 - The inward and outward: their qualities,
attributes symbols and ethics

Both the inward and the outward are rooted in day-to-day living. With regard to the inward, we have said before that you cannot do your job as a seer unless you regard the universe as a friendly place. In other words, your attitude toward the world around you must be one of trust. You have to trust the good auspices of being with regard to yourself. It is only once you trust that the light will not hurt you that you will be able to keep your eyes open and therefore see it. Your trust enables you to submit to the radiance of the world, to be awe- struck by it, and grateful for it. From an existential point of view the proper demeanour of the self with regard to the world is therefore one of trust. The world is not a wild monster about to ravage you; it is benevolent towards you.

At the same time, outwardness is also rooted in day-to-day living.

For the outward to be generous and radiant it has to leave its place to come to where you are. In other words, it has to leave itself behind. This implies leaping from the known into the unknown, which is a step of courage.

In a sense all action is a leap from the known into the unknown. As soon as movement occurs, there is change, newness and strangeness. By its very nature, the objective universe celebrates newness and creativity bearing witness to the courage of being. Your birthright is the appreciation of this extraordinary occurrence which happens from moment to moment in day-to-day living. The price you have to pay for claiming your birthright is your sense of self-importance, of bio- graphical consequence. This brings us to the final depiction of our scheme (fig. 5.4).

	Inward (The observer)	Outward (That which is observed)
Quality	Awe	Majesty
Attribute	Submission	Power
Symbol	Moon	Sun
Ethics	Gratitude	Generosity
Roots	Trust	Courage

Figure 5.4 - The inward and outward: their qualities,
attributes symbols, ethics and roots.

The description of the outward has probably made you more and more uncomfortable as it progressed because it became increasingly anthropomorphic. However, this development is important because it allows us to make the next link.

So far our discourse has reflected only one side the human being, namely inwardness. What makes the human being truly extraordinary though, is that he is inward and outward at the same time. As the observer you will always stand at the centre of your universe and be surrounded by everything else. At the same time, however, you are part of that outwardness surrounding me. Although I may possess evidence that you, too, are an observer, I can never demonstrate this absolutely. Not even the most intimate moment shared with someone you love can ever allow you to say with absolute security that you have seen the world through the eyes of another. So, while I assume that you are also an inward, to me you remain primarily outward. This means that you have both qualities: inwardness and outwardness. What is truly fascinating is that your inwardness and outwardness are in equilibrium – the one is enabled by the other.

Let us look at the relationship between trust and courage to illustrate this. In our team-building workshops one of the standard exercises involves getting the group to form a circle. One of the members is blindfolded, led to the middle of the circle and requested to fall down. After a moment of hesitation this person usually summons up the courage and launches himself forward, only to be caught by a member of the group.

This exercise demonstrates the relationship between trust and courage. Before launching himself forward, the blindfolded person is usually quite apprehensive, and even scared that he will not be caught because he does not know for sure if he can trust the group. Only after he has summoned the courage to fall can the group members demonstrate their trustworthiness. This proves that if one does not have the courage to take the risk of acting contrary to your fear, you cannot learn trust.

Nobody can demonstrate his trustworthiness unless you take the risk of trusting them with something that could be injurious to you. By doing the courageous thing, i.e. falling, the person in the middle discovered that he could trust his colleagues. So the outward act of behaving contrary to his fear enabled the correct inwardness, which is trust.

On the other hand, once he has found out that he can trust his colleagues, falling down a second or even a third time is much easier. Just as acting courageously enables trust, trust enables correct outwardness, which is courage.

Implicit in all of this is transformation. Correct inwardness transforms the outward, and correct outwardness transforms the inward. The human being in balance is therefore not static, but is forever changing, continually in transformation. He is always becoming more than he was before, becoming greater than he was one step ago.

Just as trust and courage enable each other, so do gratitude and generosity. It is the grateful heart, the full heart that overflows, that can be generous and has something to offer. The other side of this coin yields be a wonderful surprise: acting generously on the outward enables gratitude. The implication is that gratitude (contentment) is not based on things that have been accumulated, but on what has been given with generosity.

The contented are not those who have preserved themselves, the contented are those who have expended themselves. They are not those who have arrived, they are those who have departed. They are not those who stay the same, they are those who are forever chang- ing. Ultimately you do not become more because you withhold, but because you expend.

And when you are generous and give of yourself, you are of service, which means that your inward state is one of humility. You do not consider being to exist to serve you. Instead you understand that you exist to be of service to being. Inward authenticity, i.e. the sense of submitting to the other and to his good fortune and of existing to give, is recognised by others. People realise that you are genuine, they trust you and so you become powerful.

We have said before that humble men are powerful men, whereas men with an inflated view of themselves are ridiculous, irrespective of what they may be able to do to other people. When your inwardness is submission, you outwardness is powerful, and your being a miraculous metaphor for existence because your outwardness is majestic while your inwardness is in awe.

The promise here is that if you act in accordance with correct outwardness, your inwardness will be transformed. Be courageous and generous and you will be powerful and majestic. Furthermore, you will discover the treasures of trust, gratitude and contentment of heart. On the other hand, by ensuring that your intentions are trust-worthy and humble and based on a fascination with and gratitude for existence, you will become powerful, majestic, courageous and generous.

You can have it all because you actually have it already. You are the centre. The price you have to pay is your own ridiculous sense of self-importance.

Chapter 6

TECHNOCRACY: THE CRITERIA, THE CITIQUE

The Criteria

Parenting provides a very useful metaphor for the job of the leader, or the job of power, because it is the first relationship of power to which the human being is submitted. There is much we can learn about the nature of a relationship of power by examining the issue of parenting. In the simplest terms, any parenting relationship implies two parties, a big one and a small one. The big party (the parent) is the party of strength and its job is to protect the weakness of the small party and to create the conditions necessary for growth. Thus the role of the powerful one is to create the conditions required for the weak one to become big. This means that the job (or function) of power is empowerment, i.e. to elevate the one subjected to that power. If the powerful does not enable, empower and elevate the powerless, the relationship of dominance maintained over the subordinate is essentially illegitimate because it does not achieve that which power is supposed to achieve. It does not unleash the subordinate, it does not permit the actualization of the subordinate's potential.

Growth is closely associated with learning. The child's world is relatively small, with boundaries circumscribed by the presence of its mother. The home is very much the known world of the child and whatever extends beyond the boundaries of home appears to be massive, foreign and threatening.

Growing up essentially involves a perpetual testing of the boundaries of the known world, so that more and more of that which was previously unknown may become known. In this way the domain of the child is extended. The child's curiosity about that which is on the other side of the fence is therefore an essential force that exerts pressure on the boundaries of the known world to expand and become ever greater. This process by which the unknown becomes known has a number of important qualities.

First, the unknown is grasped by relating it to that which is known. The expansion of the child's world takes place from the centre of his domain. Every foreign thing that becomes familiar does so because the child has integrated it into his domain and related or connected it to its centre. In a sense he took that which was strange and separate, or "out there", and brought it home. The moment this happens the foreign element is no longer uncomfortably different, because by bringing it home the child has appropriated and befriended it.

In this sense it is true to say that growth involves befriending that which used to be frightening. Like all friendship this transformation implies a sense of empathy, of having integrated the new thing into himself so that he can find himself in it. This sensation of recognition already implies a sense of: "Ah, but I know this, it is with me."

By bringing the new friend home the child implicitly states that the friend is no longer separate, that the separateness has been overridden by oneness.

The pressure on the boundaries of the known is not accurately understood if it is regarded as bringing about a simple enlargement of the domain within the same boundaries. In fact, the pressure exerted on the boundaries changes the very nature of the boundaries.

Initially the fence around the yard is seen to be an absolutely rigid line of differentiation between the known and the unknown. But then, one fateful day, our young Ibn Batuta discovers the gate or even a hole in the fence and slips out into the street. The fence, which until then was considered to be an absolute divide between the known and the unknown, is found to be permeable because it actually allows one to escape.

Growth therefore implies an understanding of the fact that the boundaries separating the known from the unknown are not rigid and absolute; they are subtle and permeable. Furthermore, the bigger one becomes, the more subtle these boundaries become. However, this discovery can only be made if young Ibn Batuta has the guts to slip through the gate. Should he lack the courage to go out and take a look at those scary things in the street, he would effectively ensure that he remains locked in behind the gate.

Growth requires courage and one of its essential attributes is that the facile and rigid approximations of distinction become ever more subtle.

The role the leader is supposed to play in enabling the smaller person can also be understood in terms of this metaphor. Perhaps it was an older brother who took Ibn Batuta by the hand, opened the gate and lead him through it to go and play in the street. The reassuring presence of someone bigger therefore not only made it possible for the child to venture outside, but also to spend sufficient time in the street to familiarise himself with it. The result? The street no longer appears to be quite so unnerving to young Ibn. The bigger person is able to do this because he has gone through the gate many times and feels quite secure in the street. In this manner bigness enables bigness. By implication a leader can only make others big if he himself is big.

If leadership is about big people empowering smaller ones, it is very important for us to understand what power, i.e. bigness, really means.

Being big involves a number of important attributes. First of all, a big person can never be a coward; he must be brave enough to live continually in the face of the unknown. The elder brother who led Ibn Batuta into the street could do this either because he has already passed through that same gate and into that particular street before, or because his experience of other gates through which he had passed make it possible to go through that particular gate by analogy. The fact remains: at some stage or another he had put to test his fear of that gate or of gates in general, either on his own or under the guidance of a someone bigger that himself. Having faced that specific facet of the unknown he was in a position to assist someone else in doing it. Facing the unknown is associated with handling risk, or coping with the possibility of annihilation. In its most elevated sense facing the unknown means living in the face of death, or turning the terror of living in the presence of the unknown into a friend. In this way the inevitability of the unknown becomes the known principle, and every new day is engaged from the point of view that it can only have anything to offer if it brings change.

The ultimate statement of change is death, and therefore accepting change also means accepting that one of your new days will also be your last. In fact, for all you know today may turn out to be that day. This knowledge is inextricably bound up with greatness, or humanness. It is the capacity to face death in good faith, without panic and with dignity, that is the mark of the great soul.

Bigness also implies a sense of subtlety, an ability to deal with ambivalence and a patience born from the understanding that nothing is to be summarily dismissed as irrelevant, because recognition or oneness may be found there.

In a sense smallness means to be held closely, within tight boundaries. Much is viewed as separate, different, strange and threatening and is therefore to be negated, to have its consequence denied. Many things are considered to be neither of me, nor of my being.

By contrast bigness indicates a knowledge that the boundaries are not rigid, but permeable, that they are not obvious, but subtle. The "big" person therefore withholds himself from making easy pronouncements about the worth of others, or about his own traits by saying things such as "I am like this and not like that". Things are rarely exactly this or exactly that. I may be the most ill-tempered man, yet you would find that I have acted with considerable restraint in a number of taxing situations. So I, too, am not exactly this or that. I am not rigidly defined, I too am subtle, which means crass qualification like "He is always in a bad mood" is untrue.

This is why one values humility as a key attribute of the truly great person. Such a person does not have an inflated sense of self-worth based on biographic fantasy. Greatness reflects a knowledge that, rather than being a mark of consequence, the continual accumulation of biographic detail demeans one because it structures and rigidifies the self to an increasing extent. In fact, to truly face the unknown, there has to be a real sense of leaving behind that which is known. One's sense of self-importance is invariably based on a sense of "what I have achieved" which, by definition, is the known.

Along with the quality of humility there is also an implied empathic demeanour, born from the finding of oneself in the other. This implies a capacity for listening, for allowing the other to unfold, rather than immediately imposing categories which are probably irrelevant, thereby forcing the other into the boundaries of the known.

Referring once again to our metaphor, categorising the other amounts to an attempt to make the street fit into the yard, instead of leaving the yard and going out into the street. This distinction is crucial, because it introduces the essential element of care. The point is not to demean the other by making it equal to or smaller than the self, but to rise to the greatness evoked by the other. Going out means affirming the other, being of service to the other, rather than consuming it.

Martin Versfelt makes an important point in this regard. According to him the symbol of evil in all the art of the world is a gaping maw. This amounts to a statement that perversity is the view that the other is there to serve the self, that the other is to be brought into the self, or consumed. What we are saying, is that greatness implies an understanding that the self is there to serve the other and that, rather than through annihilating or consuming the other, the self grows by going beyond its boundaries to serve the other.

In a sense we may view biography as the known, comfortable yard where we are holed up. The fence of the yard is formed by our idea of ourselves. Leaving the yard means leaving our biographies behind. You do not bring the street to you, you go to it. You do not take, you give. From this point of view, largess is not based on what you accumulate, whether by way of biographic detail or possession. Rather, it is based on what you leave behind or give away.

This introduces the idea of generosity. Your greatness is not based on what you get or take, but on what you give. Accumulating in whatever form only serves to make the fence even higher, to introduce a fantastic notion of being impregnable and invulnerable which reduces everything to the safe and the known. Growth only takes place in the face of the dangerous and the unknown.

Growing up therefore implies refraining from getting the other to affirm and serve the self, while the self affirms and serves the other. By implication the correct attitude towards domain (i.e. that to which you have reached out) is custodial. Your domain is not a resource for you to consume. It is entrusted to you for your care.

Leaders are those people whose domains contain other people. The leader's custodial duty towards those in his domain is to enable them, to create the conditions in which they are able to go beyond themselves and be victorious. Essentially this means that the task of leadership is to enable generous and courageous people who are able to take the risk of acting for motives more elevated that self-interest.

The making of generous people is not necessarily a kind process. For example, it may be appropriate to drag a child who is scared of the street through the gate and into the street despite his kicking and screaming. One must be extremely careful not to equate care with a sloppy, liberal notion of softness. In fact, some forms of taking are so rapacious that they require swift and draconian retribution. In enabling greatness the leader may therefore from time to time have to act in ways that seem downright cruel. The key criterion here is whether it is done to enable the growth of the other and not to serve the leader's own needs.

A true leader has to embody the following qualities: humility, empathy, patience and fortitude in the face of adversity, generosity, care and a consequential fairness that will not allow anyone to be purely self-serving. It is of crucial importance that these qualities are not merely the product of stylistic finesse or behavioural skills learned by practice. These qualities are the attributes of true greatness.

The Critique

These criteria make a very important comment on the current idea of greatness and the associated leadership. In the current view people of consequence are defined by what they have rather than by what they give. Success is related to the size of the executive's car, the size of his budget, the size of his house and the length of his title. As a result, those who are supposed to be free, and thus in a position to free others, are themselves trapped in the fantasy of their own importance. A friend of mine called Salim has a fascinating tale that illustrates this point very well. He works for a chemical company in Newcastle that has been going through very deep waters for the last couple of years, which resulted in substantial retrenchment. The retrenchments took place in four stages, two of which affected blacks only, while the other two stages affected more senior white employees.

Salim, who is black, said that although the blacks who were retrenched were not happy about it, they responded to the retrenchments with a sense of resignation. After all, if you live simply, losing your job is not the end of the world. You can always make do somehow.

The whites, on the other hand, reacted very badly to the retrenchments. Most of them went to pieces in a most undignified way; in fact, two of them even committed suicide. They had been important, they had had company cars and lived in houses financed by company subsidized loans. Suddenly all this was taken away from them and they became nothing. So we see that these people, who were in fact small and enslaved, had this odd notion in their heads of being free, whereas those whom we normally think of as being oppressed were in fact closest to being free.

The moral of this story is very important, because it demonstrates that our current cosmology is utterly barbaric and rests upon premises that are the opposite of how things should be. It is the slaves, those who are small and terrified, who are currently in command, whereas those who have something to offer in terms of true nobility are the subordinates. Instead of the social project being commanded by the courageous in order to enable victorious nobility, it is commanded by the terrified whose sole concern is their own safety, the achieving of which is based on diminishing others.

Those who are actually small are regarded as big and therefore constitute the leadership of our age. To all appearances they are big men and they certainly have the trappings to prove it! But what happens if the trappings are stripped away? All that remains is a petrified, self- serving little person. The leaders of our time (who should also be the most noble and courageous of our time) are ruled by fear. Even worse, this fear is exclusively defined by the most base and meanest acquisitiveness. The truth is that an appearance of being big hides actual smallness.

Presenting an image that does not accurately reflect the true state of being obviously contains an element of deception. This fraud permeates every facet of such a person's life, including all his transactions. In a fraudulent transaction, an ignoble and self-serving motive is presented as a generous motive ostensibly aimed at enriching or enabling the other. Such a transaction is not about authentic giving; it is about taking, camouflaged to resemble giving.

In a leadership context this is rather disturbing. If one argues that the function of the big party in a relationship of power is to make the small party big, then the very hiding of the so-called big party's smallness is a subterfuge not to enable and give to the small party, but to take from and disable it. There is something extremely sinister about this. It is like parents who do not feed their children but rather feed on their children. The current cosmology is not at all uncomfortable with this state of affairs, since it regards the role of the subordinate, the child, as having to satiate the acquisitiveness of the superordinate.

The technocratic world view is savage in that it is cannibalistic, it consumes humanness. Enabled, generous and courageous people are supposed to be the end-result of the social project, and things (position, territory and commodities) are supposed to be a means to that end. For contemporary man, however, people are the means, the human resources, and the aim of the exercise is to produce things. Whereas things should exist to enable people, people currently exist to produce things. In fact, people are seen to be no different from things; they are resources, consumable things like ore deposits.

At this point one may wish to accuse contemporary leadership of fraudulent and deceptive behavior. This would not be fair for two reasons. First, these leaders themselves do not have any idea of which criteria to impose on their own situation.

Second, even if they had access to such criteria their description of material context and, more specifically, of space, has been formulated in such a way that the idea of place is itself a fantasy. People employed by Anglo American might work in the same building as employees of Hoechst. Although they rub shoulders every day, they regard each other as outsiders, as not of their "place". This distinction between "them" and "us", between "thereness" and "hereness" has nothing to do with physical space. It originates and exists in the mind only; it is a hallucination. Therefore, a description of the place where the manager exercises his charge has turned the context into a place of disablement because it is unreal, it is fantasy.

In order to come to grips with the implications of all this let us look at the following:

From one point of view we can say that the role of the obvious, of separateness, of commodities is to enable subtlety. The fence round the yard keeps out the frightening other for as long as it is necessary, i.e. until Ibn Batuta is brave enough to face the street. The fence therefore exists to enable the moment when the street can be faced. Its obviousness and rigidity make possible the subtlety and ambiguity of the moment of courage.

By contrast, however, the meaningful human qualities of loyalty and nobility present the means to produce the obvious, separate- ness and commodities. The terrifying consequence of this is that the qualities of the noble human being can be reduced to the status of a resource and, as such, end up being consumed.

The savage world view regards meaning or consequence as functional, as an element in the chain of cause and effect. This view implies that people use language, act as transactors in the marketplace, and functions as leaders purely because of self-interest, because they want to accumulate, to make the fence higher and higher.

What we are proposing is that meaning is not functional, but that function is meaningful; that the obvious is the cup and the subtle is the wine. We are given the world to make possible the heady intoxication of a victorious facing of terror.

This point of view has some really interesting consequences. Our metaphor of Ibn Batuta suggested a relationship between courage and an increase of domain. In other words, we may say that extending beyond territory or space is one of the manifestations of largesse, of courage. There are really two types of people of courage, namely the warrior and the pioneer, and both types go out into the world. The savage idiom has reformulated the understanding and meaning of territory in such a manner that any true sense of being a warrior or a pioneer has become impossible. However, at the same time that the warrior and the pioneer are being relegated to the realms of the quaint, archaic and irrelevant, a sloppy nostalgia about both is unashamedly invoked in order to further savage ends. Let us examine just how this is done.

In feudal Europe, knights served lords who reigned over a clearly identified territory. The knights were regarded as inseparable from the land – they came with the territory, so to speak. If the lord on the other side of the valley declared war, the prize was – literally – the head of the enemy lord and, by extension, his territory and vassals, i.e. his fiefdom. Thus the fiefdom, was the site where courageous warriors were put to the test, and its expansion or contraction made a meaningful statement on both the courage of the warriors and the nobility of the lord. In this drama the risks were real in that they concerned life and death. Failure carried the ultimate responsibility or penalty.

In present times the fiefdom is the corporation. It is commanded by executives or corporate chiefs (the lords and knights of yesteryear), and it is the place where the peasants of our age (the workers) live out their life drama.

The corporate fiefdom, however, is unique in that it is trans-territorial. The multinational corporation transcends place, thereby making it impossible to confront on a real battleground, i.e. a territory situated somewhere between "us" and "them". Without a real battleground there can be no real battles and, consequently, the risks taken are equally unreal. No fight is a fundamental test of courage, because life itself is not at stake. The price of failure is bankruptcy, retrenchment or dismissal. The risks are not fundamental because the penalties are not fundamental. Yet the executive feigns the posture of the warrior, he attacks the market, he clinches the deal, he goes for the kill. He takes on and conquers the opposition or loses the fight. He plays at being a warrior because play is the only avenue open to him, since there are no real battlefields. Rather than being alive and run ning the risk of leading a noble life, which is death, he plays at being alive.

Should this playing at being alive not satisfy the corporate eunuch, there are always other possibilities for drama presented by the gladiators of the cinema and the sports stadium. Here he may revel in the blood and guts of others without any danger whatsoever to himself.

This "spectatorhood" (i.e. assuming the status of a spectator) conveys an important message, namely that the really meaningful life is lived by others, whether on the big screen, the little box or the sports field. You are no more than a sedentary observer. Rather than living your own movie or getting involved in your own match and taking your own risks, you remain a voyeur trapped in meaninglessness because meaning, by definition, is elsewhere.

Then there are those who attempt to get closer to "warriorhood" by pursuing a fascination with weapons or some kind of martial art. Their lot, however, is not to be envied, since they are viewed and treated as some sort of Neanderthal throwback by the hierophantic intelligentsia. Their desire to become strong and be tested for their strength is regarded as evidence of their weakness. Accusing them of being "macho" is the primary mechanism used to trap them in guilt. The easiest way to undermine strength is to make the person who possesses it feel embarrassed about it.

Finally, there are those who refuse to have their martial exuberance quelled, to be throttled, and therefore seek to fight back. Often they espouse some or other underground cause because of an intuitive recognition that present-day establishment is rotten to the core. However, their pursuit of a noble fight and an honourable conquest is doomed to failure right at the outset because their enemy is trans-territorial. There can be no broad-chested confrontation with the opposition because the opposition straddles the battlefield on all sides. Territory is irrelevant. They possess all territory, yet they have none. And so fighting is reduced to the war of the flea – an ignoble, secretive terrorist exercise where their very aspiration for nobility is reduced to a sneaky subterfuge.

Ultimately, the only warrior who stands a vague chance of being anywhere near himself is the corporate executive, since his play at being real is instrumental in the production of a balance sheet. Enabling him to become what he can be is not the point; he may keep a toy version of himself simply because it is good for business. In any event, there is not much else he can be because he has been robbed of a battlefield.

This puts the problem of executive stress in its proper perspective Nietzsche believe that in times of peace men of war make war on themselves. So the executive's heart caves in, he gets ulcers and he gets cancer – all evidence of the fact that he is a being at war with himself and therefore consuming himself.

The confrontation with space or territory is also important for another noble being, the pioneer or explorer. As our metaphor of Ibn Batuta indicated, growth implies a sense of going out into the world to discover new things. Whether the wanderlust takes you just out of the yard, to the other side of the street, the other side of the city or the other side of the world, a number of basic requirements have to be met for the experience to be authentic.

First, there has to be a real sense of leaving behind, of leaving home, of going from the comfortable to the uncomfortable. Closely associated with this is the requirement for the vulnerability – an understanding that leaving the known for the unknown throws one off balance. Therefore, for movement to be movement, the place one moves to has to be strange, foreign and new. Bearing in mind that movement to the new makes possible the expansion of the self, it follows that the stranger, the more unsettling and the more foreign the destination, the more the boundaries of the self will be tested and the greater the reward will be in terms of the expansion of the person.

Over the last few decades something extraordinary has happened to the world: it became a single village. Thus, no matter how far you go, you did not go anywhere at all. To be in Tokyo is to be in Amsterdam. The Coke is the same, the hamburgers are the same (and so is the sushi, for that matter!), the hotel rooms are the same. Since there are no frontiers to be crossed, there are also no adventures to be lived, except in the very remote and surrogate sense of being a tourist. Like the megalomaniac collecting biographical trivia to affirm himself, the tourist keeps adding new destinations to his travelogue. His story, however, is incomparably boring, since its essence is not about newness, risk and strangeness (in other words, growth). Rather, it is about sameness, the same fried eggs, sunny side up, in the same impersonal dining room that relocates itself from continent to continent.

Even if the pioneer's quest for adventure is not trapped like this, the web of science will most definitely entangle it. Scientists have this extraordinary idea that they stand at the "frontiers of knowledge", that they are "breaking new ground". Yet the ground they break is really about definitions and descriptions. My wife, who knows about these things, tells me that much of molecular biology, for example, is based on deduction. The existence of the particles being described has to be inferred because they are so small that they cannot be seen. The only real risk in this mind travel is the disrepute that results from putting forward an idea other scientists find ridiculous. The world explored by the scientist poses no threat to him; in fact, he diminishes it to the point where it becomes toy-like.

Probably the greatest danger posed by the scientist as the "new" pioneer is that the present-day pursuit of knowledge has exactly the opposite effect than that for which the true pioneering spirit thirsts.

The feel of the pioneer is one of vastness, of sweeping vistas on desolate, far-off plains, of expansion. The scientist, however, expands his horizons by going onto greater and greater detail, cutting his subject up into smaller and smaller bits so that eventually it can no longer be recognized for what it was and becomes an abstraction.

The very last thing you would find at a university is sweeping, elevating and universal knowledge. What you are bound to find is an increasing plethora of departments turning sub-sub-sub-disciplines into sub-sub-disciplines which in turn become sub-disciplines which in turn become disciplines. So we have an increasing number of professors who are becoming commensurately ignorant. One of the things that fascinated me as a student was the degree to which professors of the human sciences, the supposed experts on the problems associated with being human, lead absolutely debased and immoral lives.

Therefore the redefining of space and territory has closed off the avenues whereby the grappling with space can itself become the context for taking on one's life project and assuming greatness. With territory – the primary context for self-realization – having been made irrelevant, the two archetypes relying on territory for self-realization, namely the warrior and the pioneer, are left with hollow parodies of themselves. Their playing at being themselves is tolerated since it is functional in the production of things. However, should they come anywhere near who they actually are, they would become extremely dangerous to the current establishment, since their humanity would fly in the face of any social project that has as its aim the production of things, and the diminishing of people to that end.

It is apparent that the current equivalents of both the pioneer and the warrior assume the form, rather than the content, of these roles. The corporate executive, for example, executes the directive of the board or the council of lords. However, all the battles are fought on and with paper, and bear no relation to the heroism of an authentic struggle. It is all sham. The tourist pioneer is equally the plastic replica of the original.

Once again we are brought face to face with the insight that the image of largeness actually hides smallness, and that wherever this happens the consequences are always fraudulent. These so-called big men are supposed to give us meaning by telling us about great feats of courage and of things strange and wonderful. Yet what they do is steal our meaning by trapping our attention in tinsel that has no substance. Because the savage establishment has no authenticity of its own it survives, in a sense, by cannibalizing the authenticity of others. While I was working in the mining industry, ERPM experimented with recruiting a number of people from the local township. They wanted to see if the dependency of the mine on migrant labour could somehow be decreased. However, not one of the local recruits stayed on the mine for more than six months. They were just not tough enough to shovel rock in a stope for eight hours a day. However, what this really said to me was that the rural people were a bit closer to a sense of warriorhood. They were sufficiently large in themselves to deal with an existential confrontation as fundamental as working in a South African deep-level gold mine. The township dwellers, on the other hand, were no longer close to themselves, they had been swallowed by the amorphous township existence and they just did not have the necessary stature to deal with living so close to death in such a crude production environment.

So, the industries producing the primary products that make the rest of the world run can only really do that as long as there are people capable of getting very little while giving very much in terms of personal cost. These people are just not created by the savage world view; instead, the savage world view creates people who play at being great. However, authentic greatness is needed to produce primary products, and to that end naïve rural people are employed from Guatemala to Carletonville.

Eventually these rural people get restless because, like any resource that gets used, they get used up. They lose patience and revolt. This leaves management with two options: They either have to be more subtle in their manipulation to keep the workers in the stopes, or they can move on in search of a fresh batch of authenticity to cannibalize. The latter option will mean that the entire world will eventually be populated by consumers who all watch CNN, eat Italian pizza and drink American Coke, and view themselves as modern and free.

This brings us to the function of the global village. In a sense the purpose of this pax technologica is precisely to render the authenticity of the foreigner useful to the machine – the machine can survive only as long as there are pockets of interesting humanity left. Being parasitic the machine lives by sucking life from its host, but that very sucking destroys the host and so new hosts have to be found. Eventually, all possible hosts are infected and one is faced with a massive destruction of the host population. And the next day the world will end.... They will have the beads but they will have bartered their souls.

The new savages were once seen to be magnanimously dispensing progress, but they were actually sinking the parasitic radicle so deeply into the flesh of the host that the host eventually mistook the intruder for his own self.

Against this background it comes as no surprise to find so-called nationalists in Africa, Pan Africanists, espousing democracy and socialism, ideological frameworks as European as Marx and Engels. They feel much closer to these perspectives than to the legacy of, for example, the Red Kings of the Zulu nation. And yet they still insist that they are "being themselves".

This is why you have to take care not to reduce your understanding of human greatness, and therefore leadership, to a set of behavioural refinements. There is no "how to" in greatness, there is only greatness. We have said, for example, that there are a number of important attributes associated with leadership. We have named humility, care, empathy and a capacity to listen – all of which have behavioural attributes. The danger, of course, is to confuse the attributes with the essence, thereby assuming that greatness can be acquired by mimicking certain forms of behaviour.

Much of what is considered to be politics succumbs to this weakness. To start off with, the very idea of politics is contrary to the thesis on power that we are advocating. Power is about big, grand people making others big. The powerful are there to empower, to enable others. However, the very idea of engaging in politics already has a feel of manipulation about it. Politics is about establishing dominance and position in pecking orders, about tactics, in other words doing the right thing at the right time, about withholding or giving input to one's own advantage. Politics is most certainly not about enabling others; it is about enabling yourself by disabling others. Within this framework of reasoning there is a lunacy that says: "If they are weakened, I am strong. So, the more I manipulate them, the more I make the ground beneath them fluid and throw them off balance, the more powerful I am." So, rather than enabling others, politics is about disabling others, using them only in so far as they fit in with your tactical game plan.

The skills employed to this end include smiling at pensioners, listening intently to television interviewers and kissing babies in public. All these things make the politician appear to be the servant of the people, the one who always puts his own interests second. In the mean time the slick politician is serving no one but himself, and we know it. While pretending to give he is actually grabbing; while pretending to be enabling and calling forth meaning in people's lives by reaching out, he is actually taking advantage of their good faith in order to secure a victory at the polls. Despite a carefully managed image of grand largesse, the actual transaction is not about enabling you at all, but about demeaning your life, about reducing it to meaninglessness so that the clown on the podium looks as if he is the only one of any consequence. No wonder that we become cynical and repeat after each other the depressing refrain of "Power corrupts and absolute power corrupts absolutely", just like a group of unhappy old men gossiping while feeding the pigeons in the park on a winter's morning. And no wonder that we invoke the democratic principle to provide us with the checks and balances needed to protect us from these monsters. This, however, is fatal. The fact that the puny politician uses his position to diminish you does not mean that controlling him (i.e. diminishing him so that he cannot get out of hand) will make you big. In fact, this is obviously not the case.

The small one cannot become big by making the big one small (which is really the essential perversity behind rebellion, from the Reformation to Oedipus). The only result that can be accomplished by diminishing the big guy is illustrated by the current state of affairs in many American schools: the teachers no longer beat the kids, the kids beat the teachers.

Another implication is that you can only be enabled or be called to your greater self if you have entrusted greatness to someone else. If you insist on keeping your superordinates small, you will remain small. Honour them, enable and ennoble them, and you will fly.

In so far as our current understanding of democracy is about checks and balances, it is not about power at all, but about control. It is not about bigness, but about smallness. In fact, representational democracy as it currently stands has nothing at all to do with power, and everything with control. It does not even offer a system of control with regard to the actions of the powerful; rather, it is a mechanism by means of which the truly powerless assume a façade of power. Properly speaking, representational democracy is a rule of succession. It determines who will assume the throne and for how long. It does not look at what the person does while occupying the throne; it merely restricts his access to the throne.

If we understand legitimate power to be about elevating people, the procedural arrangements in terms of which an individual ascended to the throne actually have very little to do with whether he is doing his job. Kings can enable, so can generals, dictators, or elected presidents. The rules of the tactical game which landed the person with his bum in the butter have very little to do with whether the powerful one is doing with his charge what he should be doing. I am forever amazed at one-dimensional Americans who think that the government gains legitimacy through the vote of the people.

The current understanding of democracy may probably be viewed as a systemisation of one of the attributes of power. As we have already indicated, good powerful people listen, they attend to those in their charge because they care and are interested in elevating them. This element of listening can be regarded as synonymous with taking council. Even Machiavelli encouraged the princes of Renaissance Italy to seek wise council.

Today this is known as participative management, which means obtaining inputs with regard to governance from the governed. This is considered to be the good etiquette of leadership, but it is of value only if it reflects the conscious, uncoerced good intentions of the superordinate. If it comes from the superordinate it is an expression of his greatness and as such it cannot but enable. However, if participative management is imposed on the superordinate it is the expression of his humiliation and therefore an accusing finger pointing at the ignobility of those who humiliated him.

From this point of view I think it can truly be said that present-day man in savage society is probably the most pitiable, trapped, diminished and warped human being of all time. He is probably much more of a slave than he would ever care to admit, and certainly more of a slave that many of his owned ancestors who lived in previous centuries.

Living in a machine world presupposes regulation. In fact, the job of governance is considered to be primarily legislative. This means that all the members of a democratically elected congress or parliament aim their resources at one thing and that is saying "NO". As if the Ten Commandments do not suffice! Not only shalt thou refrain from stealing thy neighbour's handbag, thou shalt not park in the wrong place, or allow thy dog to bark too much, or keep a sheep in thy garden, or slaughter a chicken for thy consumption. It is astounding to discover how many innocent activities are actually criminal offences. These days you stand a better chance of getting away with murder than with selling unpasteurized milk from thine own cow!

The primary attribute of our current enslavement is the fact that one of the major projects of the technocratic state has been to disarm the citizen. The most heinous crime is to take the law in you own hands, because you are supposed to let the police handle it for you. So, while you are disarmed the only people who are armed are the functionaries of the state and outlaws – both of which pose a threat to you. This image of democratized man as an emasculated, powerless being is carried to such extremes in many Western democracies that even daring to submit your child to corporal punishment is considered a criminal offence. Compare this with Mosaic man who, in terms of the law, could literally kill his own child if he so wished. So this so-called primitive was man enough to be entrusted, literally, with the lives of other people, whereas modern man cannot even be trusted to care for his dog. Consequently we have to fund the SPCA to make sure that he does this properly.

The diminishing of the human being in savage society does not stop with his political emasculation and the denial of authentic leadership, but also has a social, an economic and an existential facet. An examination of economic transaction, for example, shows that the same themes are borne out. All economic transaction ultimately has to do with enrichment. If you have something that someone else wants, and they have something that you want the two of you swop and voilà!... both of you have been enriched. By exchanging something less preferred for something more preferred both parties are richer than they were before.

This criterion of enrichment becomes more subtle when one side to the transaction is represented by a medium of exchange. There is a difference between a transaction that strictly involves barter (goods for goods), and one where there is a definite seller (the one with the goods or services) and a buyer (the one with the money). In an ordinary barter exchange both parties are simultaneously buying and selling. With a medium of exchange, however, the buyer and the seller have a different status, and therefore the transaction is somewhat more complicated. There is a clear distinction between the selling side (the giver) and the buying side (the receiver). This difference is borne out by the fact that it sounds odd to say "I'm taking tomatoes to the market to buy money". So, while the general rule of a barter transaction still holds true, namely that both parties to a transaction must leave the transaction enriched, a more subtle subrule is added as soon as a medium of exchange is introduced.

Trying to formulate this subrule, we can say that there is an added moral obligation of service on the side of the person selling you something. As soon as money is involved, there is a generous side to the transaction, represented by the seller, and a grateful side, represented by the buyer. The price the seller gets for his goods or services is actu- ally a statement of the reward (the grateful "thank you") the buyer gives him for being well served. So, the role of the seller is to serve and enable the buyer, and not the other way round. The seller fulfils the generous, giving side of the transaction, and the buyer the grateful receiving side. Once these two moments are in place the transaction does what it is supposed to do: it adds value, it enriches, it makes the participating parties bigger at the conclusion of the transaction that they were before.

Transaction is therefore a metaphoric terrain for the enabling of humanness. Just as battlefields enable courageous warriors to take risks and expand themselves, so markets are about making people bigger, about enabling them to become more than they appeared to be. However, this can happen only if both parties to the transaction honour the principles by means of which value is added.

The view that the seller has to serve the interests of the buyer gets much lip service, and we constantly hear that businesses have to be customer focused, that the customer is king, and so forth. Still, we know that the bottom line (profitability), is the real reason most bussnessmen will cite for being in the market. They are not essentially there to serve a client or to give him something. They are in the market to maximize their benefit from the client, to get as much as possible from the client while giving him as little as possible. Although they pretend to be customer focused, in reality they are self-focused.

This is certainly particularly true of the current state of affairs in the marketplace. A bank advertisement, for example, would promise customers heaven on earth, with sufficient credit facilities to acquire anything from a new car to a trip to London. The bank manager is portrayed as compassionate and friendly, a personal "friend in need" who is only too willing to open his palm and let the beneficence of being itself flow forth to you. Of course the advertisement makes no mention of something we only know too well, namely that no bank manager is so daft as to give you all this for nothing. In return for his benevolence he wants security, a handle on your house, a guaranteed statement of your earnings and, more than anything else, he wants his money back – with interest. If you should ever dare not humour him in this respect he will take you to the cleaners. He will sell your house for R10 and still hold you accountable for the outstanding debt.

We all know that behind the appearance of benevolent generosity there hides a lethal predator, and yet we continue with the charade. All the pretence about enriching us is really about our being bonded, indebted and impoverished so that they may be enriched. They say they are giving, yet they are taking. They say they are enriching, yet they are impoverishing.

We have said that the selling side of the transaction is also the generous side; if you serve me well and appropriately, I shall reward you handsomely. My payment is therefore a reflection of my gratitude for the generous service you rendered. However, for this to occur I must be genuinely enriched, I must be more than what I was prior to the transaction, I must be greater.

Transaction today is about doing exactly the opposite. The bank appears to make you greater; after all you have graduated to a bigger home. However, the truth is that you only appear to own the house because it is bonded to the bank. Your bigness is an illusion, and it is based not on your elevation but on your diminishing. You are indebted and weak. The house that should be a source of solace, secrity and strength for you, is actually something that keeps you awake at night worrying about meeting the payments in the event of losing your job.

The practice of creating a need for a product or service through deception is not restricted to banking. In fact, it is applied in everything regarded as marketing by savage society. Once again, the idea is not to provide you with something you need, thereby making you more fulfilled and stronger. It is about creating a need in you for something, in other words to make you feel discontented, weak and poor, so that the seller can be enriched. Sellers embark on marketing to weaken and impoverish buyers, whereas sellers should actually strengthen and enrich buyers.

Nothing is sacrosanct to sellers in their quest for power over buyers. Beautiful young bodies and exotic island getaways are exploited to sell alcoholic beverages. Now, in my experience, the consumption of strong liquor is not at all related to a Caribbean wonderland of neverending romantic sunsets, but to fathers beating the hell out of mothers on a hot Saturday afternoon while bedraggled kids, wide-eyed with terror, scuttle for the temporary safety offered by a neighbour's house. This is not the stuff that dreams are made of, it most certainly does not ennoble; on the contrary, it debases – utterly.

We must understand that there is no way in which the island imagery can elevate the actual baseness and ignobility of the domestic violence of hot Saturday afternoons. Instead, the island is debased by being connected to the commodity precipitating those horrific events. Try using a wonderful thing to elevate a base thing, and what you achieve is not the ennoblement of that which is base, but the debasement of the noble.

So we see that what is noble, beautiful and elevating is appealed to, not to give people something, thereby elevating them, but to take from them and debase them. As a result people become cynical of the seller's motives and, even more disturbing, of all that is elevated. The Banana Board, for example, produced an advertisement for bananas that featured the opening bars of Beethoven's Fifth Symphony as a jingle. The music was "performed" by a group of kids dressed up as bananas, singing the word "BANANA" ad nauseam. Beethoven himself said that the opening bars of his fifth Symphony depicted "the knocking of destiny at the door". The Banana Board had it used by a group of prancing children in fancy dress to sell bananas. They ruined Beethoven's Fifth for me for all eternity, because every time I hear the motif, I see a mental picture of a ten-year-old camouflaged as a banana mindlessly miming "BANANA".

The really disturbing thing about all this is that there is just about nothing elevated or elevating that has not been sullied and tarnished by these marketing ghouls. Fatherhood, motherhood, love, companionship, friendship, strength, courage, beauty, honour – to name but a few – have been used to sell anything from toothpaste to condoms. Base things are dished up in such a way as to appear elevated. Taking is dished up as giving to the point where the so-called intelligentsia consider taking to be the motor that makes the world go round, and anything more noble than that to be romantic nonsense.

Ultimately, the rugged, adventurous image of a victorious cigarette smoker is the painted fact of a little grey man laughing all the way to the bank and, to add insult to injury, he is not even doing it for himself, he is doing it to get a pat on the head from his shareholders. The whole thing is a fraud and we know it. It is about a little man selling us a fantasy of meaning, of consequence, not to give us anything at all, but to grab from us and devastate us before making the great escape. Viewed against the fundamental criteria for elevating the other, it is revealed for what it is: a tool for debasing the other. The real tragedy of this whole process is that the elevating things which could make the human condition even remotely tolerable, are brought into disrepute.

One could say that the equity of a transaction can only be celebrated if there is a process of negotiation or bargaining. It is through bargaining that balance is achieved between buyer and seller. In a sense negotiation ensures that the seller is appropriately rewarded, i.e. to the degree to which the buyer has been enriched. One can go even further to say that without negotiation there can be no guarantee that the transaction will do what it is supposed to do, namely enrich both buyer and seller.

Savage society has succeeded in effectively undermining this, because the consumer typically does most of his shopping in a supermarket or at chain store where the status of the buyer vis-à-vis the seller has undergone a number of important changes. First, the feeling that buying is a human transaction has disappeared. Supermarkets became successful precisely because they took the human ingredient out of shopping. In days gone by the buyer was served by the seller in person: the shopkeeper behind his counter. Nowadays you simply serve yourself, ostensibly in a demonstration of your totally self-sufficient independence. There is no longer a sense of needing to interact with another human being in order to be enriched. By its very nature this kind of interaction was – and always will be – hard work because it involves an exchange of energy between two people. Luckily this is no longer necessary. So, we can remain equal to the worst in ourselves while acting out our little acquiring soliloquy without being confronted by another human being.

However, this surrender of the hard work and the responsibility to take on the seller in order to ensure that the transaction remains equitable came at a terrible price: the freedom and independence of the buyer. If you want to put this statement to the test, try taking on the cashier at the checkout point next time you shop at a supermarket. After she has rung up the goods, look her in the eye and calmly make her an offer of, say, 20% less than the amount she asked for. At best you will be gently requested to leave the store – without the goods and without paying – because of your unseemly, rather childish behaviour.

So, for doing that which any adult buyer must do if he takes on the responsibility of transacting, you get treated like a child. On the other hand, if you behave like a child, accepting the nature of the transaction in subservient acquiescence, you are considered to conduct yourself like an adult. For behaving like a helpless idiot you get treated like a sane adult; for behaving like a sane adult you get treated like a lunatic. "It's a strange, strange world we live in, Master Jack!"

Chain stores are enormously inventive in their exploitation of the childlike status of clients, for example by rotating the specials offered at different branches so as to confuse the client as to prices. One day Item X is ridiculously cheap and the next day it is hideously expensive. This strategy creates a sense of confusion and disconnection with regard to price.

The system of pricing by means of barcodes takes this principle even further: unless you possess astounding powers of recollection, you will have absolutely no idea of what you are going to pay for a commodity once you get to the till because the price does not even appear on the item. This leaves you with two options: either shut up and cough up, or vote with your feet and enter the trap next door for more of the same treatment.

As a matter of fact, the idea of voting with your feet does nothing to free you, it just underscores your undignified position. Voting with your feet amounts to communicating through a balance sheet, in other words, through dead numbers on a piece of paper. This is entirely different from taking on the opposition in a hard-nosed negotiation. Voting with one's feet leaves one with a feeling of sulkiness, of not talking, of acting like a victim. Acting in silent resentment does not make you big, it reduces you to insignificance.

Probably the most serious area of discourse with regard to trans- action in the savage society concerns currency. Without exception, all currency in the world today is based on a promissory principle. In other words, the act of payment actually constitutes only a gesture, a promise to pay, rather than a substantive exchange. If you pay some- one with paper money, and he returns to demand that you make good the promise to pay the amount indicated on the paper, you would yell at him not to behave like a fool because he has his payment in his hand. Yet, what he has is not payment, but a promise to pay. Take a R20 not from your purse and scrutinize it closely. You will discover that it states that Dr. Stals promises to pay you (the bearer) R20 if you present your paper note to him at his office in Pretoria. Take him up on the offer and see what happens.

To fully appreciate the implications you need to consider the fol- lowing facts. Five centuries ago a man would go to the marketplace with some gold in his hand to buy something. The gold he carried in his hand made a statement about him: it said he was a rich man, a big man. In a sense it underscored his sovereignty as a transactor. Gold was a commodity in its own right that required human effort to produce. It could not be manipulated because there were numerous sources of gold, and anyone could produce or transact in it. The supply of gold was not judiciously controlled by some "gold supply manager". In fact, there was no such manager. The gold in you hand therefore affirmed your wealth. There was no referral to a system straddling you that defined the value of what you had in your hand.

Today a man goes to the market with paper money in his pocket. Now, you may well ask: "So, what's the difference?" The difference is that the manager in control of the press that prints the notes could go mad and speed up the printing process, thereby halving overnight what the man has in his pocket. Although the transactor appears to be wealthy and big, he is in fact small, since his status of being big is conferred on him by the people who manage the system. Destroy the system that defines his wealth and he is impoverished. If the system is mismanaged by the few technocrats who are in charge, a whole nation can become bankrupt. So, whereas in the past people had their own wealth in hand in the form of gold, people today have only a representation of wealth (the promissory note), which implies that their wealth is conferred on them by the authority that issued the note. Therefore it is the system that is wealthy, and the individual is its bondsman. Every transaction the individual makes by means of paper money affirms the authority of the system with regard to the definition of wealth which, by implication, takes that authority away from the person himself.

Our current understanding of economics is to blame for much of this illness. An economy is understood to be a system of interacting forces such as market forces, exchange rates and interest rates. Graphs and trends are considered to be the real things, whereas they are actually a representation of the real thing. They are the magical aggregate of actual, individual transactions between real people.

We have already established that a transaction is legitimate only if it enriches of elevates both parties. Viewing the economy as a systemic phenomenon has the effect of relegating to irrelevance this moral criterion because morality is applicable only to sentient humanity. Trends are things and as such can be neither moral nor immoral.

In our examination of the political and the transactional frameworks of savage society we have found that, instead of doing that which they are supposed to do, i.e. elevate and enrich people, they do exactly the opposite, they debase and impoverish. However, the spoor of this debilitating disease are not restricted to the streets and the markets, they lead right into your house. In order to verify this statement, let us take this discourse, literally, closer to home.

One would assume that people would have an almost primal, intuitive understanding that marriage is about kinship groups, about children, about clans.

In short, marriage is about people. It is an alliance between a man and a woman that is inextricably associated with raising people from babies. Not only is the familial project people, it is also the making of big people, the raising up of people.

Our current view of marriage is somewhat different. Rather than its being about two people battling to provide the best for their kids, it is now about a couple battling to pay off the bond, the hire purchase contract on the car, et cetera. In fact, these demands are so enormously time consuming that there is precious little left for children, and so to have more than two kids is considered to be sheer lunacy (as well as environmentally unfriendly).

Marriage is therefore no longer a collusion of two people that has as its aim the raising up of people. Instead it has become the collusion of two people to acquire things (property). The project involved is things, and human qualities (such as love and care) are functional only in so far as they can serve the Great Acquisition. To fund this unedifying project both mother and the father are marched off to the labour market, while the children are left in the care of an institution such as a school or crèche.

It is particularly with regard to the mother that this practice has enormously serious implications. The raising of children, or enabling of people, is not considered to be interesting, whereas the making of things is regarded as stimulating, because it is in making things, savage society maintains, that meaning is to be found. Consequently the young people are left in the care of the thing (an institution), so that the older people can go and expend themselves in the service of the production of things. The young are in the custody of things and the old are servants of things. People are therefore less than things.

The image is one of imprisonment, with the human being confined to structures of which he is the subordinate. It is most certainly not the image of the human being that we have drawn and come to appreciate, namely a towering giant rising above his status as thing, and assuming his true nature of always being beyond, greater than and over the thing. Oddly enough, most people consider this utterly undignified quest for acquisition to be for their children's sake. This point of view cannot be defended. Of what use can the accumulations of a lifetime be to a person who is alive only in a metabolic sense because the qualities of humanity have never been nurtured in him as a result of neglect? Instead of being successful parents in the true sense of the word, his parents made a success of paying off the television set. In fact, one could say that the savage home is thoroughly uninhabited. Nobody is ever at home. The parents are at work and the kids are at school. No wonder that women flee this cotton wool suburban nightmare. It has no meaning because it is empty, there is nobody home. It is a place of loneliness and despair, and it is perceived as utterly meaningless because it is not directly involved in that which has meaning in the savage world view, i.e. making things.

The populated home is not functional to the savage social project because the project runs on people's acquisition. Populated homes are expensive to run, and besides, it is becoming increasingly expensive to send all the brats to school. Money spent on the kids cannot be spent on bonds, or new video recorders or anything else that we regard as progress. And if expanding the family by way of having more kids is considered to be irresponsible, taking in an aged parent is seen to be stupidly sentimental, and the contracting of polygamous marriages is nothing short of criminally insane. I am always fascinated by the reaction of so-called progressive ladies upon discovering that one of their worker comrades has two or more wives.

The family in savage society is weak because strong families are detrimental to the technocratic project. What if the father or mother gets transferred? The whole lot needs to be uprooted and transplanted in another spot. Very inconvenient to everybody concerned. Coming to think of it, marriage itself is an inefficient and inconvenient arrangement, since it does not allow both parties to pursue their brilliant careers to the best of their abilities. We had better get rid of marriage. Perhaps we can even eliminate the necessity for ovaries and conduct all reproduction of the race in a culture medium.

Even when the inhabitants are physically present in the home they are still absent in many cases, because their attention has been caught by the one-eyed electronic monster squatting in the corner. Every day at work their being is subordinate to the things they have to produce. From work they go home where they slip into a somnambulant fantasy, reducing themselves to things, nothing more than unconscious bundles of peristalting guts and popping synapses.

The television screen is savage man's closest companion. It provides solace when he is unhappy, partners when he is randy and harmless excitement when he needs to get the adrenalin flowing. It is educator and parent to his children, spouse to his wife and the final arbiter and dispenser of all things good and truthful. He gives it his undivided attention and rapt devotion because it is his window on all things of meaning. And while his attention glues him to the screen he is totally unaware that his teenaged son is shooting up in the loo. In fact, he only discovers something is amiss when the ambulance comes to collect the body of the young OD victim. The extraordinary thing about all this is that one actually sympathises with such parents: "Ag, shame, what a terrible thing...." However, if the child had died from some other form of neglect, such as withholding food or medical care, we would clump together in front of our screens voicing our indignation when the scoop is splashed. "How can anybody do something like that?" we would ask.

Therefore, the current vision of man is that of a diminished, frightened being. All the arenas that should enable his largesse serve to disable him. He is trapped within and reduced by himself, because as a human being, as a person, he is regarded as nothing more than a biography, a sad tale of woes dragging through life which becomes steadily worse and more menacing. As a result, he regards himself as getting more and more defined, more and more concrete, more and more thing-like.

The last fact he has to face is that, far from getting more settled as he gets older, he moves closer and closer to his own death, to absolute transformation. Although he thinks he is getting closer to stasis and arrival, he is in fact hurtling towards total change and final departure. Anything that reminds him of this, the inevitable outcome of life, is carefully sanitized.

Death and disaster happen to the images on the TV screen or to the statistics in the newspaper. They bear no relation at all to his own life. If anything, they are proof that his life is untouched, that nothing has happened to him. He is safe and secure, he is sure, ensured and assured. He does not even have to face his own dead, they are taken care of by the undertakers before being swallowed by the earth. He may wish to see the body once it has been properly dolled up, but this is regarded as being a trifle perverse. It is just so much better to leave the coffin closed.

Current man is not big, he is most tragically small. In addition, he has very little hope of ever becoming big because those in whose charge he finds himself are as small as he is, if not even more minute. This establishment is run by the terrified and perpetuated by terror. Its overthrow is not only inevitable, but absolutely necessary because the world is dying of neglect in the hands of these terrified dwarfs. Our environmental problems have nothing to do with controlling resources so as to prevent them form being depleted and everything to do with enabling large people who will take care of the world and give to it, instead of steadily consuming it.

For The New Man

Having examined the status of the human being in the technocratic tyranny, it is very easy to succumb to despair. Everything seems to indicate that this juggernaut cannot but self-destruct, destroying all of us in the process.

In a sense this is the embodiment of the triumph of the savage world view, this very pervasive feeling of emasculation and futility that is underscored by the nature of everyday life. The key to over- throwing this barbarity does not lie with a structuralist party with a programme and a proper agenda because no party can free the human being. Only a human being can free the human being.

The answers do not lie elsewhere, they do not form part of the never-never fantasy of movies or television, where it is someone else who does the heroic deed. You have to be the hero, you have to do the heroic thing. You have to overturn the nature of your everyday experience.

It is men and women who will make men and women. If our current world has reduced all people to boys and girls, it is up to you and I to be the people who can change this, since we are the ones who have come to understand the nature of the monster we are dealing with.

The very first step in reclaiming our lives is to affirm them. Your life is meaningful. The gladiatorial design of the savage world reduces us to meaningless spectators on the periphery; the centre, meaning, belongs to the Great Ones on TV, or the exalted ones at the apex of some pyramidal structure. This is itself is a lie because the conscious, observing human being is uniquely and perennially at the centre of things. This is the truth, also at this very moment. This is not fantasy.

The most important thing to remember is that, for you, the other is that which surrounds you. It stands before you like a mirror reflecting who you are. So, take a close look at that which confronts you now, at this moment. Ask yourself how you can help, how you can contribute. Then proceed to act according to the best of your understanding, with courage and generosity. If you do this, you will change the nature of the world that you are in.

Never allow yourself to be disarmed by the size of the problem. The bigness of the problem is in itself a hallucination.

The only thing that exists for you at this moment is that which is around you.

Go, take care of it and be free.

Chapter 7

THE MAKING OF MASTERS

E arly in 1982 I made an attempt to account for the discontented, the "victim" in the organisation who feels oppressed and believes that those in charge have only their own interest at heart and are in the relationship to maximise their own benefit at his expense.

One of the discoveries I made about the victim is that because he feels that he is being treated unfairly, he thinks that it is legitimate for him to get as much out of the relationship as he can while giving as little as possible. The victim is therefore a taker.

When we tried to account for victimhood and discontent we found that the root of the problem was the attitude – or values – of the manager. The question then arises, "Who is this manager who turns people into victims, and what does one have to do get him to offer appropriate and correct leadership to his people?"

This is followed by a closer look at some of the senior managers with whom we worked between 1989 and 1992. I hope that this examination will put us in a position to distinguish between the kind of manager who creates victims and the kind who does what a leader is supposed to do in the way it should be done.

We shall also look at what happened at Safripol, which was an exercise in turning managers into leaders.

Let us first turn to the question of who creates victims. We have stated that the victim himself is a taker simply because he knows that those in charge are taking from him. The only question that filters down the hierarchy of the organisation to reach the person on the shop floor amounts to tapping a finger on the bottom line. "Where is my production?" asks the manager.

It is interesting to reflect on the attitude of the manager making these demands. For instance, the demands become louder and the manager more panic stricken the closer one comes to the threshold of financial viability. These demands are made because the manager is scared and feels himself to be weak and at the mercy of other, larger forces.

Therefore the manager himself is a victim. Victims create victims. A colleague, Eben Meets, came across a very good example of this phe- nomenon. He was senior personnel officer on a mine in the Orange Free State when a shift boss from an adjacent mine was temporarily appointed mine overseer.

The shift boss – let us call him Jaap Fourrie – had an excellent track record and also a mine overseer's ticket. Dave Scott, the section manager of the shaft, allocated a particularly difficult section to Jaap with the promise that if he made a success he would receive a permanent appointment as a mine overseer. The task assigned to Jaap Fourie was well nigh impossible, and the other mine overseers on the shaft frequently warned him that he would come to grief. During these exchanges, which mostly took place in the change house (the mineworker's confessional), Jaap would be fiddling with his shoelaces, a tiny, superior smirk on his face. The impending promotion was very important to him since it would earn him a company car and a B-type company house. In the Welkom community these were powerful status symbols.

Jaap tried very hard to make the grade and worked hard at his relationship with his shift bosses. Eventually his attempts at winning them over got out of hand and spots of good cheer were doled out with abandon after shift in his office.

True to his word, Dave gave Jaap a permanent position as mine overseer and Jaap got his sought-after company car and B-type house. However, unknown to Jaap, a process was being set in motion that would have devastating consequences for his recent elevation to the better life.

The mine came under pressure from its regional office to improve production. The mine manager, looking for a subordinate who could be relied upon to deliver the goods, focused his attention on Andy Seal, a production manager and Dave Scott's boss. Seal, a graduate and an immigrant, boasted an impressive track record and was one of the corporation's identified high-flyers. With the new demands on him, as well as a reputation and a career that had to be protected, Seal was soon knocking at Scott's door, demanding more. Scott was quick to relay this pressure to his mine overseers, and in particular to Jaap Fourie, who was not yet producing the tonnages he had promised. The result was a radical change in the relationship between Jaap and his shift bosses. Suddenly, the friendliness and the joviality were gone. Keenly aware of the risk to his newly achieved status, Jaap put extreme pressure on his shift bosses to deliver. Even if a shift boss had a perfectly legitimate reason for failing to produce, such as collapsed haulages, Jaap was unsympathetic and unreasonable. "Don't dump your bloody problems on me!" he would yell at a fleeing shift boss who had been trying to explain why he had not met his production target. "I want call, not your feeble excuses!"

Quite understandably, the shift bosses response was to "sprag" (frustrate) Jaap as much and possible and consequently, Jaap's section began to fall apart. Jaap was not doing for them what a person of power should have been doing. He was not interested in them, only in what he could get out of them.

At this stage we were doing an investigation of this mine, and I met Jaap. One of the requirements of this specific job was that Volker and I had to go underground with every mine overseer to get a first- hand feel of his section.

Visiting Jaap's section was a harrowing experience. He was extremely suspicious of us and obviously felt that we had been sent to spy on him. In fact, we got the impression that he was hoping to get rid of us by deliberately putting our lives at risk. He took us into an unusually hot section with very poor ventilation, and made us crawl through panels without water for hours on end. At the end of our ordeal Volker was displaying symptoms of severe dehydration and I was feeling rather light headed.

During this punishing rush around Jaap's section, the prevailing poor morale became as clear as daylight. We passed a drinking well constructed from a 44-gallon drum – with a hole in it. When I asked Jaap how the hole had come to be there, he informed me that he had punctured the drum with a four-pound hammer because he had found a horde of "boys" at the drum having a "party" (with water!) instead of being at work in the panels. Bear in mind that this place was as hot as hell!

Obviously, the less Jaap produced, the more he came under pressure from the top. He, in turn, got increasingly unreasonable with his people who, consequently, gave him even less. In the end, the rock just stopped coming from Jaap's section. Very soon, this *madoda* (big man) lost his *stepis* (promotion). He lost his car and was put into a smaller house, and then he was chased back to his previous job like a caned schoolboy. The man was destroyed.

We have seen, in the most concrete terms, how victims create vic- tims. From the mine manager down, we see have seen how careers, securities, reputations and rewards are invoked by fearful superiors to squeeze more out of their subordinates. We have also seen how the ability to perform and produce is negatively affected to a degree directly proportional to that to which unreasonable demands are made on people. If this kind of behaviour takes place throughout an organisation, total collapse is the only possible outcome.

In his sullen slavishness, the victim will only give, albeit grudgingly, while a whip-wielding overseer is in direct attendance. The more we use control and fear, the more we apply the whips of status, security and reward, the more we consume each other. This is what Martin Versfeld calls mutual cannibalism. Nobody gives, but everybody takes. We are devouring one another.

If one of our major concerns is to create wealth, we must understand that this can only happen where people are giving to each other, instead of taking from each other. This means that the generation of wealth cannot be successfully pursued by someone who is a victim. It is masters, people bearing the profoundly human qualities of will, courage and generosity, who create wealth. Our primary concern must therefore be with the making of masters.

Just as victims create victims, it is a master who makes masters. A master is the leader who, out of the substantiveness of his person, is genuinely concerned about his people. Such an ethical and generous human being unlocks the capacity to give in his subordinates because he cares. It is by his care that he nurtures the frightened victim into becoming a generous, giving masterly person. The crucial point about the masterly leader, then, is that he empowers. He unleashes another's capacity to give, and he does this by giving.

I have an example that accurately demonstrates this process. It happened on Virginia 2 Shaft, Harmony. We originally started working on what was then known as the East Division of Harmony, which included Virginia 1 Shaft (V1), managed by underground manager Jon Dudas, and Virginia 2 Shaft (V2), managed by Ollie dos Santos. Both men reported to a section manager called Bob Atkinson.

At the time, V1 was doing reasonably well and although very important shifts took place there, I shall rather focus my account on events on V2.

V2 had been under call for 24 months, meaning that the shaft had not met production targets during this period. Morale on the shaft, from the underground manager down the ranks, was exceedingly poor. To exacerbate the situation, relations between Dos Santos and his boss, Atkinson, were very strained, since Atkinson basically regarded Dos Santos as an idiot who did not know the first thing about mining.

After some exposure to leadership themes, the mine overseers on both shafts were asked to indicate the problems they had in providing good leadership. The list of complaints they produced was staggering.

On V2, for instance, the following issues were raised:

- Overcontrol by management
- No participation in decision-making
- Poor production incentives
- Senior management solve problems personally
- Lack of parity in status of service departments
- Management manages by fear
- Fringe benefits (cars) used as a whip.

When these complaints were presented to the managers in the division, they reacted with shock and surprise. Afterwards, Atkinson admitted to me that he had had sleepless nights as a result of the information put forward. He and the underground managers were totally unaware of the degree to which their behaviour was turning their mine overseers into victims. The subsequent change in behaviour of management was dramatic. Atkinson immediately stopped interfering with Dos Stantos's running of the shaft. This was obviously painful and difficult for him to do because it meant that he was no longer in control of every movement on the shaft. Instead, he had to entrust the running of the shaft to Dos Santos.

Dos Santo was faced with a similar crisis. In the past, he had exercised very tight control over his mine overseers; now he had to let them run their own divisions in good faith that they would not run amok once they had the reins in their own hands. He was able to do this only because Atkinson was no longer breathing down his neck. Dos Santos now turned his attention to addressing the concerns experienced by his mine overseers.

The response on the shaft was staggering. Within the first month of addressing these problems, V2 "shot its call". After this, production improved incrementally every month to the point where, six months later, V2 mined 28 000 m2 of reef whereas it had a call of 25 000 m2. Thus, once the leadership problems at senior level had been resolved, proper conditions could be created for the men who were actually doing the work to extract more rock from the earth. How was this achieved? I shall explain by way of a story relating to a mine overseer on the shaft, a man by the name of Mike Nelson.

Mike Nelson went on leave at the time a major restructuring was taking place on the mine. His section and underground managers were replaced by a single person, the shaft manager. This man, Piet Ludick, put the men under a lot of pressure, presumably because he was new and therefore somewhat insecure.

Nelson's division came under close scrutiny since it was here that a new mining system, known as non-electric blasting, was experimented with Angus Pretorius, the shift boss who was standing in for Nelson during his vacation, was totally incapable of withstanding the pressure coming from Ludick with the result that Nelson's division started falling apart.

When Nelson returned from leave he was furious. He held Preorius responsible and threatened to "hang him up by the ears!" Fortunately for Pretorius, the other mine overseers on the shaft rallied around him and informed Nelson of Ludick's behavior.

A few days later, Nelson did not go underground. Instead, he went to Ludick's office for a proverbial "man to man" behind closed doors. Nelson told his immediate superior that their job as leaders on the shaft was not to grind their people. Rather, their job was to care for their people, to give to them so that they would be capable of giving as well. The result of this interaction was that Ludick relaxed the reins and V2 production became even better than it had been.

This anecdote illustrates how masters make masters. Right at the outset, Bob Atkinson and Ollie dos Santos had the nightmarish task of relaxing their hold on the mine overseers and entrusting the job to them. This meant that they had to courageously confront their fear that the mine overseers would mess up the job. Furthermore, they had to act on a whole list of complaints presented to them by their mine overseers. What was asked of them was to care, to give and to be courageous. In fact, they had to be masters.

By being masters, Atkinson and Dos Santos created the conditions which enabled Mike Nelson to risk his security by confronting his new superior in defense of his crew. It was this kind of masterly behavior that made it possible for ordinary team members on the shaft to produce more than they had ever done before. And so they, too, became masters.

By comparing the stories of Mike Nelson and Jaap Fourie, it is possible to make a number of observations about the nature of the master and the victim.

First, it is important to understand that the master is characterized by power, whereas a victim who is in a position of authority will always invoke control. The master is powerful because he merely needs to make his requirements known to his subordinates for them to rush to fulfill them. This is authentic and legitimate power. It is a giving and generous.

The most important attribute of power is that it reproduces itself. Power generates power. What characterises the master is that he entrusts his subordinates with power. The mine overseers on V2, for example, were nothing but a group of bleating victims, until their two managers, Bob Atkinson and Ollie dos Santos, had the cour- age to entrust them with the power to do their jobs and therefore stopped controlling their every move. In return, the mine overseers gave to these two men unswerving loyalty and delivery over and above that which was required, beyond the wildest expectations of either of them. We see, then, how the master, by empowering his subordinate, unleashes him, making possible the most exciting developments. In fact, power is the only mechanism by means of which the human project may be released from a grey sentence of drab drudgery.

The victim in a command position will be concerned with control because he cannot trust. This is inevitable because a victim fears. Jaap Fourie, for example, was solely concerned with the impending loss of his newly acquired status. This proves that the victim is essentially a miserly being, purely involved with himself and his own concerns. This self-centred focus means that the victim is essentially concerned with his own consequence. The easiest way to gain consequence is to take it from one's subordinates. Thus, instead of acknowledging the consequence of his subordinates and thereby empowering them, he turns his subordinates into fools. The reasoning behind this is: "If they are less, I must be more."

The attention of the subordinate, in turn, is fixed on his own uselessness. By focusing his attention on himself and his inadequacy, the task is forgotten. Ultimately, the job cannot be done and wealth cannot be created.

Thus the victim is a taker who steals the consequence – or meaning – of others because of his fear. He fears the loss of his job, his reputation, all those arbitrary things surrounding him which he has constructed himself. Consequently, his entire life is structured around a central fear of discontinuity, of loss, of death. From this fear he enacts the Pharaonic building of structures that will enable him to live, forever. He prefers to remain eternally frozen within his self-constructed casing rather than taking the real risk of trusting, of empowering. After all, if he should do that, things may go badly wrong. They may even come to an end!

This shows up another attribute of the master. The master is able to risk, and it is because of this that masters are associated with the creation of wealth. Johnny Rech, then Manager of Elandsrand, once told me that there can only be profit where there is risk. How true! The master can take risks because he has a fundamental trust in the good auspices of Being. He is a trusting being, he knows that "everything will be OK, in the end." Therefore, it is not difficult for the master to make decisions. He is courageous, and there is nothing indecisive about him. This courageous decisiveness is what sets masters apart, what makes them so exciting to be with. In this regard I would like to share an inspiring testimony about a Mr Olivier from Genmin. The man who told me about Mr Olivier said working for him was like riding a huge wave. Because decisions are taken there is always a risk involved, but there is also movement, life.

Wealth is generated within a relationship that is dynamic, like life itself. It is the nature of life to explode, to increase *ad infinitum*. The master celebrates this very nature of life.

In contrast, the victim cannot make decisions because he cannot risk. So he grinds to a halt. His lack of faith in the good auspices of being causes him to retreat into his structured mausoleum. In his fear he must control everything. This overriding motive to control eventually strangles the very life out of an organisation.

Victims are the product of control just as control is exercised by victims. That is why it is so terrifying that current leadership language consists of the managerial idiom, which has to do with mixing and manipulating forces and is essentially concerned with control.

Control reduces people to the status of takers because they cannot be trusted to give. Forever consuming resources, they do not take only from other people, but from the world itself. So, the more we teach our young leaders the language of control, of employing the surrogate, the more we hasten the demise of our world. The more controls we invoke, the more we create the conditions for taking. The effect of all this is much more comprehensive than merely undermining the generation of wealth. It actually amounts to a brutal and crude ravishing of the world.

In this regard Martin Versfeld has given us a category which is even bigger than that of mutual cannibalism, namely the "rapist society". And if you should ask him to explain to you exactly what it is, he would point out its signs plastered all over our world, from the semi-clad billboard poppet, draped over a car to the financial institu tion offering you a *bond* to set you free! The overriding message is that you are weak and incomplete, that life will only start if you consume a certain product. Take, little children, take!

If mankind is to make it successfully into the 21st Century, the social project should involve the making of masters, of people who have something to give. In other words, people have to be restored to their rightful place at the centre of the social project. However, this will only come about at a price, i.e. the removal of that which currently occupies the centre: production. Whereas a sane society would use things to enable people, our society uses people to produce things. Furthermore, in the process people are reduced to the status of things. This has to be redressed. An essential ingredient of this reversal must be to disseminate an understanding of the difference between power and control among those who are in charge in order to establish legitimacy.

This is a formidable task, and the responsibility for realising it lies with the ordinary people – you and I – and with our leaders. We all share in this responsibility because it concerns the minutiae of our day-to-day existence. We must find, and celebrate, the heroism of daily living. As this century draws to a close, it becomes critically important for us to accept and enact daily the challenge of living in a substantive, generous and ethical manner.

If we should fail to do this, we will be faced with grey, sarcophagal, structural extinction. Be courageous! Remember that the generation of wealth and, indeed, life itself is the fruit of risk. Risk-taking is the very nature of the courageous and generous master. The master can afford to live dangerously because he trusts Being.

The Story of Safripol:

Introduction

Our first serious attempt at establishing these themes in an organisation took place toward the end of 1990 and involved a company called Safripol. I had been invited to do a presentation to the man- agement team of Safripol at their annual management conference. The invitation resulted from a presentation I had done for a group of Sentrachem human resources managers earlier that year which had been attended by the training manager of Safripol, Richard de Swart.

At the stage I knew nothing about Safripol but subsequently I learnt that it was managed by Sentrachem and that it was one of the major producers of plastic in the country. The plant was situated in Sasolburg and employed about 600 people.

After my presentation I was asked by Duncan Blackburn, the man- aging director, for an appointment to discuss the situation at Safripol. In the course of our meeting he raised two issues that were of primary concern.

First, a quality programme that had been launched about three years before had failed to realise the envisaged benefits. According to Blackburn this was the case because employees did not trust management and therefore seemed to view the system as nothing more than a manipulative ploy.

Second, he was gravely concerned about tensions between black and white employees on the plant, especially since Sasolburg was an ultra-conservative community and a number of white employees were members of the AWB. Shortly before they had built a new, integrated staff canteen which was attacked by white right-wing employees who refused to share canteen facilities with blacks. In a subsequent letter to me he described Safripol at the time in the following terms:

Casting my mind back to 1990, January, when I became Managing Director of Safripol, I think I would, without prejudice to the previous incumbents to the post, summarise the Safripol climate as follows:

1. We were a task-orientated company, concentrating on getting the job done, with little true understanding of interpersonal relationship dynamics. Foremost in this regard was our Quality Process, in which we were attempting to bring about a culture change without the knowledge of all the factors required, especially with- out understand the leadership roles of the main players.

2. We suffered from a lack of cohesion within and between teams within the organisation, resulting in high frustration levels, especially in middle management, in turn resulting in *inter alia* a poor perception of the executive as a cohesive and purposeful team.

3. Leadership role clarity was lacking in management and supervisory levels which in turn added fuel to the above fires.

After deliberation and discussion of the central arguments, it was agreed that the following broad strategy would be embarked upon to address identified issues.

First, we would conduct a survey of the climate of employee opinion in order to identify the levels of trust in management on the plant and to isolate the key areas of employee discontent.

Second, we would train two groups of senior line managers (managers reporting directly to the executive) to enable them to conduct a leadership workshop for their subordinates in their own departments. These "training of trainers" workshops for senior managers would take place over days, at the end of which the managers would be asked to identify key problem areas in the organisation that prevented good leadership from being exercised.

Third, we would take the executive away on a four-day workshop during which the following issues would be discussed:

• Leadership (essentially the same content as that which senior managers had been trained to deal with)

• Trust among members of the team, and a mutual assessment of each other in terms of the leadership criteria

• Diagnostic materials (both in terms of feedback from senior managers and the climate survey).

The aim was to formulate a strategic plan to address the problem of employee discontent and leadership on site.

Fourth, we would undertake regular feedback sessions to discuss progress with various leaders on site.

Content

Both the workshops and facilitation efforts focused on the difference between managing and leading. The perspective put forward incorporated the following four major themes:

First, on the basis of my research on mines I concluded that there was no correlation between employees' granting or withholding trust in management and the "rewards" the received. For example, I found very high levels of trust in management in situations where people were poorly paid and subjected to appalling conditions. The criterion in terms of which trust was granted or withheld concerned the attention given by the manager to the well-being of the employee. This personal interest was put to the test when an employee approached the manager with a problem or grievance. The criterion for granting or withholding trust was more absolutely and stringently applied the more powerful the manager was seen to be. This link between power and the degree to which criteria are applied, indicates that the criteria used by employees to "measure" management are those used to measure power. This should actually come as no surprise since the workplace is characterised by the exercise of power as it is manifested by management's demanding of delivery. These criteria indicate that the manager has no right to demand delivery on the basis of rank or the fact that the workers receive remuneration. He has this right only if he shows personal care for his people and does not regard them purely as resources, i.e. the means to an end.

Second, in most work situations the manager sees the point of his activity to be a growing balance sheet. What he therefore cares about – and is expected to care about – is numbers, and people merely become a means, a resource to be used to this end. The crux of his relationship of power over his subordinate therefore does not lie in enabling him to the greatest possible extent, but rather in what he can get from his subordinate. The natural result of this is that the subordinate becomes discontented because he feels used. In order to deal with this discontented employee the manager normally solicits the assistance of a surrogate functionary in the guise of a human resources manager or a similar expert. The role of this surrogate with his specialist expertise is to act as a stand-in, to provide a secondary or proxy function to deal with employee discontent so that the leader of the enterprise remains free to pursue the "real" business of maximising profits. Therefore, the business of the enterprise leader is not to enable people, but to make things.

Third, the manager on a gold mine draws X units of timber from a timber yard, Y units of machinery form a store and Z units of labour from his hostel. He mixes these according to a formula he learnt at business school, throws the resultant mixture down a hole and produces gold. The whole approach is pure alchemy – something for which the same man would have been burnt at the stake not too long ago. Why? Because he obviously does not understand that gold is not produced by some magic formula, but by people who are courageous and noble enough to go into extremely dangerous places and blast out inaccessible rock. What actually produces the gold is thus not XYZ, but human generosity. This means that the manager's business should also not be XYZ, but enabling human beings who possess courage, nobility, chivalry and generosity. The tragedy is that in treating people like consumable resources the manager makes them feel used, thereby causing them to become fixated on their own needs. Instead of making generous people who will give of themselves and produce a surplus, he makes victims who are extremely concerned with getting what is due to them because they are being abused.

Fourth, if our society is to be transformed in any essential sense, it will be because leaders in the workplace are serving and enabling their people while dealers in the marketplace are serving and enriching their clients. Our current cosmology is based on a most barbaric and outrageous axiom, namely that the world goes round because of people's self-interest. This is not true. People who are here to enrich themselves and maximize their own benefit do not help the world go round, they kill it.

During the leadership workshops, these ideas were woven into a process that we refer to as the HEAT role of the manager or supervisor. HEAT is an acronym for the four essential qualities of a good leader: helper, example, advocate and teacher.

The Helper

The helper looks at the behaviour implicit in good leadership. In this respect there are two areas of relevance: first, and most important, is care. What we set out to achieve are the conditions under which the leader will understand that his role is not to tend to a balance sheet, but to enable people. What he should care about are the people who work for him, and he should entrust the execution of the task, i.e. making the balance sheet grow, to the people in his charge.

This shift of attention has a very obvious handle to it, i.e. time. If your attention is focused on numbers, that is the aspect to which you will devote most of your time. If people are important to you, you will be spending your time on them. Spending time on people has a specific purpose: enabling the subordinate to grow or, in other words, creating the conditions under which it is possible to entrust the task to the subordinate. This element can be measured in terms of structural authority. The more decisions are entrusted down the line, the more empowered employees are.

The Example

The example really lies at the heart of the HEAT role because it addresses work values. The crux is that the current poor leadership endemic in technocracy will not be changed simply by looking at behavior, because the things that are really important to people – their values – underlie behaviour.

Here it is important to distinguish between needs and values. When asked to identify their work values, people will frequently cite things such as job security or job satisfaction.

However, these are not values at all as job security or job satisfaction. However, these are not values at all because they are concerned solely with individual self-interest. Proper values always refer to things the individual recognizes as being greater than himself, to things for which he is prepared to put his self-interest second. Values have nothing to do with getting and everything to do with giving.

Honesty, for example, is a value. It is often not in one's self-interest to be honest. Honesty only becomes relevant when being honest is uncomfortable.

The distinction between needs and values is critical when one wants to differentiate between leadership and management. The manager is charged with maximising the interest of the shareholder, in other words, with getting as much as possible from the employee.

The manager's own aspirations and rewards are linked to this task since glowing balance sheets are sure to bring him promotion and rewards. His first instinct is therefore to ensure his own benefit as well as that of the shareholder. This state of affairs will only change if the manager consciously identifies proper values and subjects his own interest to those values. Only then can he start giving to the employee and stop taking from him.

The distinction between management and leadership also makes it possible to examine the difference between victimhood and mastery. The victim bases his behaviour on his need. Consequently he views the world and others as sources to be exploited for his personal gratification and understands his own sense of behaviour to be based on something he has to get from outside himself. Therefore the victim is a taker.

The master, on the other hand, understands that he has no rights and, properly speaking, is not entitled to anything at all. Mastery therefore means understanding that you are not here to get, but rather to give, and that behaviour is not conditioned by what happens to you, but rather by what you have to offer.

This distinction reveals the true nature of the leader's task: to make masters, or people who will give of themselves, and not victims, or people who will exclusively pursue their self-interest. This will only happen if the leader himself is a master because it is a master who makes masters. Victims in command can only make victims.

The Advocate

The advocate seeks to provide the leader with insight into the process of giving someone who feels that he is being defined or oppressed by forces beyond his control, a sense of control over his own life. The following piece of industrial poetry really sums up the perspective:

Victims have gripes
Masters have goals
It is your job to make masters
It is your job to help the victim
Turn his gripe into a goal.

The Teacher

The point of departure of the leader's role as teacher is that since the first relationship of power a human being experiences is that of being parented, studying this relationship may bring numerous insights about power.

Any parental relationship has two participants, a big party (the parent) and a small party (the child). The role of the parent, or big party, is to create the conditions under which the small party will be able to grow and become big.

Therefore, the job of the powerful with regard to the powerless is empowerment, and the relationship of power is only legitimate to the extent that it empowers the subordinate party.

The perspective emphasizes growth and teaching as key foci of the leader's job. In fact, it stresses that the superordinate only achieves legitimacy in his role of command if his *raison d'être* is the enabling and growth of those in his charge. The superordinate only achieves legitimacy if he is a master.

Trust

Apart from the elements of the HEAT role, a major issue dealt with during the workshops was trust, which was relevant to both the leadership theme and the functioning of the work team.

With regard to leadership, it was pointed out that the managerial approach to people was essentially one of control. Why? To ensure that employees gave the manager what he wanted. Control was essential because the manager could not trust his people to give freely, of their own will. This control implies a lack of trust. For the leader to get on with his real job – that of enabling people and giving to them – he has to entrust the task to those people. By shifting his attention from numbers to people the manager implicitly entrusts the numbers to the people.

The argument is that if two people (subordinate and superordinate) in a relationship do not trust one another, the only person who has the authority to change the tone of that relationship is the superordinate.

The Process

Our work at Safripol commenced in November 1990 with a survey of the climate of employee opinion, undertaken by Shelly Easton. She drew up the following report on views of and trust in management and supervision on the plant:

Trust in management was very positive for white employees interviewed whereas black employees expressed negative trust in management (fig. 3.1). Trust was granted to management by whites mainly because management had been seen to be helpful in the past, kept matters confidential and could be relied upon to look after the interests of white employees. Black employees withheld trust primarily because of management's lack of attention to grievances, not keeping promises and poor pay. The pay issue was seen to be one of discrimination. It was perceived that black employees were paid a minimum, whereas whites received relatively large salaries. It was also believed that job discrimination still existed, and was linked to a lack of promotion of blacks within Safripol.

Fig 3.1 - Trust of Safripol employees in management, 1990

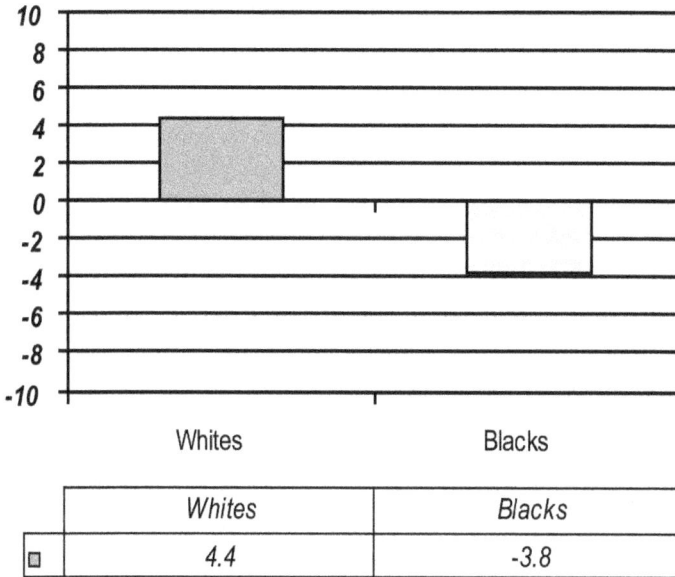

	Whites	Blacks
▫	4.4	-3.8

Trust in the immediate supervisor was fairly positive for white employees, although less so than that in management (fig. 3.2). Forty-five per cent of black employees interviewed considered their immediate supervisor to be totally untrustworthy. Overall, trust was found to be negative among blacks. The main reasons given for this lack of trust were, again, lack of attention to grievances and promises not being fulfilled.

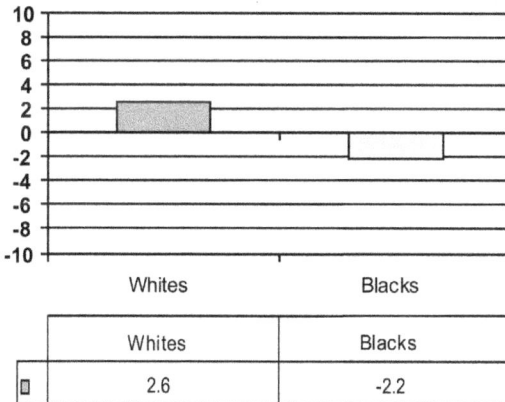

	Whites	Blacks
▫	2.6	-2.2

Fig 3.2 - Trust of Safripol employees in supervisors, 1990

Almost 70% of white employees interviewed believed that management had an interest in their welfare. Once again, management's past actions primarily contributed to this belief. In contrast, only 23% of blacks interviewed shared this view. Black employees cited lack of attention to grievances, poor pay, lack of promotion and discrimination as reasons for believing that management did not have an interest in their welfare.

The survey therefore clearly revealed a deep polarisation of black and white opinion, as well as a very poor climate among black employees. These findings confirmed the concerns that had previously been raised and, in Blackburn's own words, "...[it] created an aware- ness in [management's] minds of the need for change".

As part of the strategy to address the poor climate of employee opinion, a group of senior managers, all of whom reported to the executive, attended a leadership workshop soon after completion of the survey. At the end of the workshop they were asked to review the current leadership of Safripol in terms of whether they cared for people and whether people were granted enough authority to do their jobs. A number of issues which affected the leadership provided by management at the time were identified.

This information, along with the results of the climate survey, was worked into a four-day workshop for the executive in February 1991. The programme of this workshop was the following:

- **Day 1 and 2:** A review of leadership and an examination of the HEAT role

- **Day 3:** The issue of trust and the relationships of trust in the team

- **Day 4:** An examination of the material provided by the senior managers and the climate survey in respect of the executive. The aim of this was to get the executive to identify and commit themselves to a plan of action.

Much of the discussion during the workshop centered around the problem of control. In view of the idea that a relationship of power is only legitimate if it has as its aim the empowerment of the subordinate, it was clear that control had to be approached differently: it could no longer be viewed as an end in itself, but had to be regarded as something flexible that had to be incrementally suspended in order facilitate the growth and empowerment of the subordinate. The process of empowerment would obviously have an impact on trust, since a person who was entrusted with a matter was clearly no longer being controlled.

The financial manager, in particular, had tremendous difficulty with this whole idea. He argued that the essence of his discipline was concerned with control, and could not see how this could be changed. He was adamant that as far as money was concerned, nobody could be trusted because people would be tempted to line their pockets. One of the metaphors we used with regard to trust made him particularly uncomfortable, namely that trust was only relevant when risk was involved. If you really want to know if you can trust a man, give him a knife and turn your back on him.

The other members of the executive team were much more positive with regard to the arguments we put forward, and the workshop ended on a high note with Duncan Blackburn giving each member of the team a wooden knife as a symbol of his commitment to empower them. In Blackburn's own words, they returned to the organisation having "redefined [their] mission, vision and values into a meaningful set of management principles used on a daily basis within [the] organiser".

On their return to the plant these managers instituted a number of changes, the focus of which was empowering their subordinates. It is difficult to enumerate these changes because they were essentially associated with attitude. The essence was that the managers had to view their subordinates as people and not merely as human resources. Because of the subtle, incremental nature of this shift and the fact that almost common-sense, day-to-day things were involved, there were no enormously dramatic changes. In most cases the initial change amounted to a backing-off by the manager concerned, an approach that implied a sense of patience which demonstrated that the manager was at least considering how he could be of assistance to his subordinate, instead of simply pushing him for more. It also implied due respect to the line of command since the manager was not to get involved in the job of a subordinate by giving instructions to a person working for that subordinate.

One of the more dramatic examples of progress involves the case of Piet Cilliers, the production manager, who revolutionized his whole approach to such an extent that the change in his department was almost instantaneous. Whereas routine meetings in the past had been unpleasant affairs where the minutest details were scrutinized and criticized, he now no longer concentrated on what he was – or was not – getting from his people, but rather on how he could be of assistance to them.

On the topic of empowering subordinates, Blackburn commented that it "[was] becoming a consistent management behaviour apparent to supervisory level which [had] ... already shown a return on investment ... product quality [was] rapidly improving ... productivity [had] improved in many areas, and the impression was gained that Safripol [was] becoming a happier place in general."

It is not possible to fully appreciate the courage shown by the executive team without considering the radical nature of what they had pledged to each other. Essentially they had undertaken to change their basic premise, or sense of mission, as the leadership of Safripol. They were no longer in the business of producing plastic, or of making a balance sheet grow. Rather, they were in the business of growing people, and the production of plastic had become a means to that end. This leap of faith implied that if management took the risk of empowering ordinary people to turn them into extraordinary people, those same people would continue producing plastic thereby ensuring the financial viability of the organisation.

However, it was certainly not all plain sailing for the Safripol team. Indeed, a number of things happened shortly after the team had committed itself to this change of direction which had serious implications with regard to trust. The first of these "obstacles" was the discovery by an auditor of a number of accounting irregularities which implicated the financial manager. This came as a terrible shock to Blackburn since, in a metaphorical sense, he had been stabbed in the back with the very knife he had given the financial manager. To make matters worse, Blackburn had always considered this man to be his friend and therefore found it difficult to understand why the financial manager had not discussed the issue with him before it assumed such critical proportions.

Dealing with this problem became particularly difficult since it also commented on the issue of care. The question was raised as to what would be the caring solution in this case. There were two alter- natives: one could do one's utmost to rescue the person and save the situation but, at the same time, institute more stringent controls to ensure that it never happened again, or one could let the financial manager bear the full consequences of his actions. Eventually, a solution was found somewhere between these two extremes.

What this event highlighted, however, was that to attempt to cover for all eventualities by means of stringent control mechanisms amounted to involving one and all in the misdemeanour of an individual. The implication is that because one person has shown himself to be untrustworthy nobody can be trusted. Clearly, trust will only flourish if those who behave in an untrustworthy manner have to face the full consequences of their actions. This is not only consistent with the responsibility of empowerment, but also means that the trust that has been granted to others is not curbed.

In terms of our metaphor: because one of his team members had stuck the knife in his back, Blackburn was faced with the very real choice of whether he should claim back all the knives he had given to the executive. He chose not to, which indicated maturity and restraint well beyond the ordinary.

Shortly after this crisis a serious fire broke out on one of the plants causing the death of an employee. In the panic following the fire the plant manager, in collusion with a foreman, forged some documents in order to exonerate the foreman. The documents concerned essential routine safety checks that had not been done. The problem was exacerbated in that this manager had taken the whole issue of empowerment very seriously and had achieved some quite remarkable improvements in production. Furthermore, by forging the documents, the manager had actually attempted to protect the foreman which, it was argued at the time, demonstrated that he really did care about his people.

In the ensuing disciplinary enquiry both the foreman and the manager were dismissed. This came as a shock to quite a number of people on the plant, because it was not considered to be entirely fair. However, the motivation for the verdict was that in a climate of trust, the kind of dishonesty shown by the two men could be toler- ated. Although they could not be accused of having been responsible for the fire, the deliberate attempt to forge documentation in order to save their own skins – even if it were done in a state of panic – was inexcusable.

Safripol produces two kinds of plastic, polypropylene and polyethylene. After the dismissal of the manager of the polypropylene plant, the manager of the polyethylene plant, Jaco Kellerman, was put in charge of both plants. He is another one of the remarkable men who made the Safripol story possible.

In pursuit of empowerment, Kellerman soon did away with the clock card system. He did this because he believed that the matter of keeping time had to be handled by the employee and his supervisor. This move effectively put a large amount of discretion and responsibility in the hands of the foreman – with encouraging results. In the month before the system was abolished 17 complaints were lodged about payment for work done. In the first month of the new arrangement there were only two, and in the entire year which followed only two more complaints were made.

Kellerman also undertook a number of other initiatives aimed at empowerment. However, he subsequently admitted that not all of these had been entirely successful. In July 1991 a second fire occurred on the plant which, although it did not result in loss of life or injury, caused significant damage. At the time management voiced their concern that empowerment had possibly progressed too quickly, and that at least with regard to safety, employees were not adequately equipped to deal with their new responsibilities. In Kellerman's own opinion this assessment was not entirely unfair. He had refined his own understanding of empowerment to mean a gradual process during which each subordinate is encouraged to take on some of his superordinate's responsibilities. In the process of negotiating this growth, an opportunity is created to identify and address possible shortcomings in the subordinate's knowledge.

At the beginning of 1991, the Safripol executive team committed themselves to a course of action aimed at legitimising their leadership. In essence they undertook to focus on "growing" or cultivating people and entrusting them with the responsibility to produce their product. The year that followed was an exceedingly difficult one during which the team's commitment to their chosen course was tested under the most trying conditions. Duncan Blackburn himself described 1991 as the most difficult year of his life. It remains to be demonstrated whether the risks taken by the team were worthwhile. There are two ways of doing this. The first is to look at the effect endeavours had on the climate of employee opinion, and the second, to review their effect on the organisation's performance.

The climate of employee opinion

From 1990 to 1991 a number of remarkable shifts occurred in the climate of employee opinion. Trust in management, for example, remained very positive among white employees (4.4 in 1990 and 5.2 in 1991), but there was a substantial improvement in trust among blacks (from -3.8 to 0.4). This is depicted in figure 3.3.

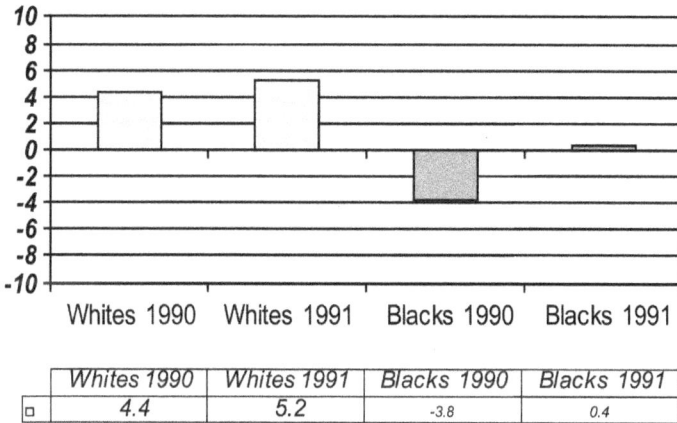

	Whites 1990	Whites 1991	Blacks 1990	Blacks 1991
□	4.4	5.2	-3.8	0.4

Figure 3.3 - Trust of Safripol employees in management in
1990 and 1991

With regard to the various departments the most significant changes occurred in production, where trust in management increased from 0.5 to 5.0, and in engineering, where it increased from -0.4 to 1.9 (fig. 3.4).

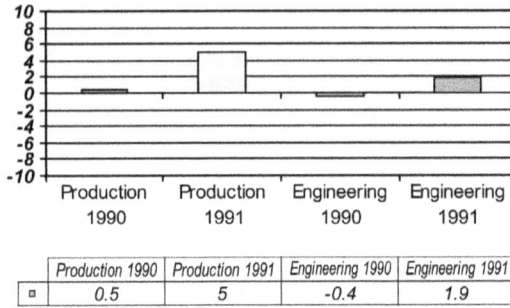

	Production 1990	Production 1991	Engineering 1990	Engineering 1991
◻	0.5	5	-0.4	1.9

Figure 3.4 - Trust of Safripol employees in various departments
in 1990 and 1991

Among white employees, trust in supervisors (fig. 3.5) improved from 2.6 to 4.8. Trust in supervisors among black employees rose dramatically, from -2.2 to 3.4.

The most noteworthy shift was in production where trust in supervisors increased from -1.6 in 1990 to 5.3 in 1991 (fig. 3.6). Also significant was the change in trust in supervisors in the engineering department (-0.1 in 1990 and 3.8 in 1991).

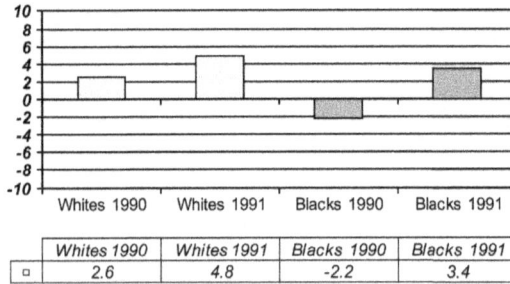

	Whites 1990	Whites 1991	Blacks 1990	Blacks 1991
◻	2.6	4.8	-2.2	3.4

Figure 3.5 - Trust of Safripol employees in supervisors in 1990
and 1991

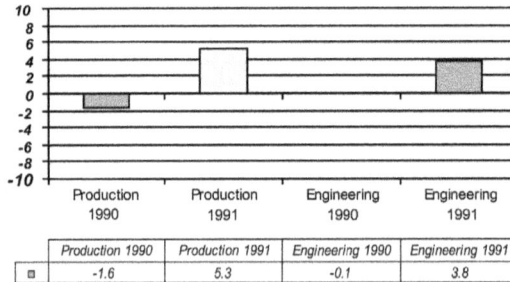

	Production 1990	Production 1991	Engineering 1990	Engineering 1991
◻	-1.6	5.3	-0.1	3.8

Figure 3.6 - Trust in supervisors among various departments of
Safripol in 1990 and 1991

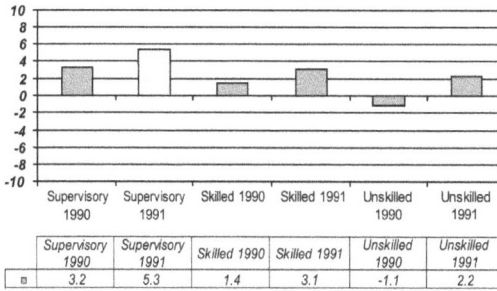

Supervisory 1990	Supervisory 1991	Skilled 1990	Skilled 1991	Unskilled 1990	Unskilled 1991
3.2	5.3	1.4	3.1	-1.1	2.2

Figure 3.7 - Trust in supervisors among Safripol employees in
various job categories in 1990 and 1991

While all job categories showed a remarkable improvement in trust in supervisors (fig. 3.7), the quite dramatic shift among technical and skilled employees deserves special mention. It improved from -1.1 in 1990 to 5.3 in 1991.

All employees showed a marked improvement in trust in the human resources department, but production deserves special mention because of an increase from 1.6 to 5.8 (fig. 3.8). This shift is very interesting since production people traditionally have a negative, even antagonistic, attitude towards the human resources department. The improvement in trust must therefore be seen as evidence of a con scious attempt by the human resources department not to assume the role of surrogate.

The implication is obvious: not only was the stature of the human resources department not harmed by their decision to avoid a surrogate controlling function, it was actually enhanced.

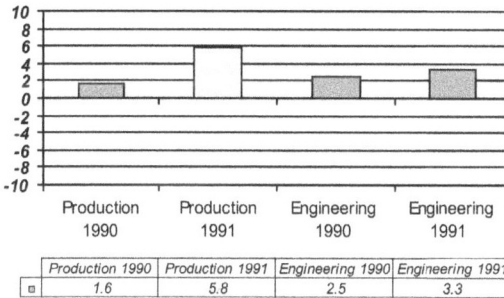

Production 1990	Production 1991	Engineering 1990	Engineering 1991
1.6	5.8	2.5	3.3

Figure 3.8 - Trust among Safripol employees in the human
resources department in 1990 and 1991

All employees' views of management's interest in their welfare improved substantially during 1990 and 1991. Of particular interest was the remarkable shift in positive response among blacks (from 22% to 51%), production people (from 38% to 77%) and supervisory personnel (55% to 100%). All these changes were highly significant since interest in the personal well-being of employees had been identified as the key criterion in terms of which trust in management is granted or withheld. That this was still the case was demonstrated by the very high trust in management of employees who felt that management had an interest in their welfare (6.9), as opposed to the low trust of those who felt management had no such interest (-5.1) (fig. 3.9).

The Results

This shift in the climate of employee opinion was accompanied by a number of changes. In a letter I received from Duncan Blackburn in August 1991, he gave a broad overview of events at Safripol, indicating that they had managed to do the following:

• Redefine their mission, vision and values into a meaningful set of management principles used daily in the organisation.

• Empower subordinates. This was becoming consistent manage- ment behaviour apparent at supervisory level, which Blackburn believed had already shown return on investment. Product quality was improving rapidly and productivity had improved in many areas. The general impression was that Safripol had become "a much happier place".

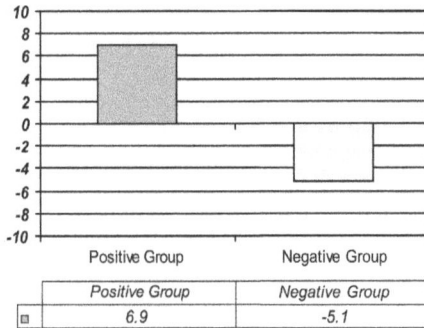

	Positive Group	Negative Group
▫	6.9	-5.1

Figure 3.9 - Trust in management of employees who felt that management had an interest in their welfare

• Management was confident that the perceived changes were permanent. The newly developed budget showed that employees were committed to the new, caring Safripol in many areas, "too numerous to list".

One of reasons for wanting our involvement in the first place had to do with the polarized relations between blacks and whites on the plant. The focus of these sentiments had been the integrated staff canteen. By July 1992 these sentiments had relaxed to the point where white employees from the polyethylene plant, who used to be the most conservative in the organisation, had made a representation to management requesting the removal of the divider between the black and white section of the canteen.

By the end of 1991 the union representing white employees had ceased to play a role at Safripol because these employees had come to believe that management was looking after them. There was a similar shift in attendance to the black union, although this took a little longer to materialize. At the end of 1990 the union represent- ing black employees had had around 96% membership at Safripol. By July 1992 this figure had dropped to 64% and was still declin- ing. It must be stressed that this decline in interest in and support for unions did not result from a management clamp-down on unions; it occurred because management was making an earnest attempt to provide better leadership, which meant that the surrogate role of the union was being steadily eroded.

Part of this overall trend of improvement included a 22% improvement in absenteeism from 1990 to 1991. The remarkable overall monthly improvements are listed in table 3.1.

Table 3.1 - Overall monthly %gures for employee absenteeism at Safripol, 1990-1991

	Jan	Feb	Mar	Apr	May	Jun	Jul	Aug	Sep	Oct	Nov
1990	144	241	281	262	184	358	170	270	316	211	236
1991	129	189	194	148	239	242	203	170	248	196	205

One of the most dramatic shifts in absenteeism for the same period occurred at the polyethylene plant (table 3.2).

Table 3.2 - Absenteeism at the polyethylene plant, 1990-1991

	Jan	Feb	Mar	Apr	May	Jun	Jul	Aug	Sep	Oct	Nov
1990	49	20	74	58	43	77	35	36	20	62	17
1991	25	28	17	1	34	16	9	11	19	22	23

Under Jaco Kellerman's leadership the process of empowerment at the polyethylene plant bore a number of fruits, which were added to by the efforts of his colleague, Marcel van Droogenbroeck, who was running the laboratory. Van Droogenbroeck described his experience of events at Safripol from November 1990 to July 1992 as follows:

1. Top management moved the focus from technical to people. People are the most important asset of any company. Treat them well and the rest will come automatically.

2. Technical requirements are still important. However, in order to achieve these requirements, communications in all direc- tions are strongly recommended. Again, technical requirements can only be met by motivated and well-cared for people.

3. Industrial leadership principles are applied by top management.

4. Applying the above principles in my laboratory have proved very successful. The last disciplinary hearing was about 18 months ago, compared with a few hearings every year.

5. Objectives can only be met successfully by mutual trust (worker-employer relationship).

6. Some statistics to prove the above:

1.1   *Laboratory sick leave*
        1991 – 1.6%
        1992 – 0.55% (up to June 1992)

1.2   **Customer Complaints**
        1990 – 103
        1991 – 28
        1992 – 8 (up to June 1992)

1.3   **Product Quality**

	PE-HD (Grade 1)	PP (Grade 1)
1990	84.1%	77.4%
1991	88.2%	82.5%
1192	96.8%	87.4%
(up to June 1992)		

This account contains a number of important facts, but the most important one probably concerns customer complaints because these reflect on the performance of the laboratory.

The role of the laboratory is to check the quality of products from the plant and to do investigative work for clients with regard to specific applications or product quality. This service was the cause of many client complaints in 1990, but by 1992 the situation had improved dramatically.

It is also of interest that Van Droogenbroeck attributes the improvement in product quality of the two other production departments, namely granulation and the polyethylene plant, to improved leadership.

Another important aspect concerns the confirmed importance of an increase in senior leadership's assistance in the process. In discussions with Kellerman and Van Droogenbroeck, both men insisted that their boss, Piet Cilliers, had to get most of the credit for these improvements because he had made it possible for them to run their own departments without interference.

Improvements were not seen to have taken place only in the production department. The logistics manager, Donald Houston-Macmillan, also accounted for a number of improvements, some of which were quite dramatic. In the past, truck standing time at Safripol, for example, was about two hours. Subsequently, employees then did a number of things to improve on this, such as staggering tea times. The cumulative effect of their efforts reduced truck standing time to 30 minutes.

The enthusiasm of Safripol employees also had an effect on the haulier, because Safripol warehouse employees started complaining directly to the truck drivers that they were too slow. The net result of employees' increased interest in their work was that the average daily number of loads per truck were pushed up from 1.6 to 2.1. This improvement alone saved the company R60 000 per month. But, there were still other improvements with regard to transport. For example, instead of letting a truck with a ¾ load go, employees started looking for ways to despatch full trucks.

One of the people who worked for Donald Houston-Macmillan was Dix Muller, who was in charge of the computer section. Muller had the following to say about improvements he had noticed at Safripol over the previous two years:

> I would say that there has been a great improvement in communication. We have management feedback sessions, and we hear everything that we have to hear. This is so because the people now trust

us, they are now talking to us. There has also been an improvement in our relationship with other departments. In the past we were of the opinion that we were the computer experts, that we knew everything and that the other people just had to accept what we gave them. They had to accept it because we knew best. This has changed. There now is a realisation that we are there to serve the other departments and that we have to give them what they want. So it is no longer a case of us giving them what we want, we now do our best to give them what they want.

Another one of Houston-Macmillan's departments that had been problematic was the canteen. He had to spend much time there because of erratic performance. This problem has now been resolved to the degree where he only has to speak to the manager in charge of the canteen for 10 minutes each month.

Houston-Macmillan has also remarked on another factor he thinks has had a positive bearing on absenteeism. In the past, if an employee had a problem he just stayed away. Now the tendency has developed for employees to approach their managers with these problems because they are assured of a sympathetic ear.

Some of the changes and improvements that occurred at Safripol as a result of our intervention were surprising. The financial manager, Willy Fryer, found that it had become easier to obtain people's cooperation. The preparation of board papers, for example, had always been a headache for the people who had to do it because they were dependent on information they were supposed to get from colleagues in other departments. Frequently it was extremely difficult to extract this information, which caused an enormous amount of stress for everyone concerned. With the changes in climate at the plant these problems seemed to have evaporated. Preparing budgets was no longer an issue, and board papers were completed ahead of schedule because other departments were so prompt in providing information. A very exciting development is that Safripol has put together their own process for relaying the new perspectives further down the organisation. This process is intended to focus the minds of all employees on certain key values by indicating the common thread of service which runs through leadership thinking. The key values are that people should give of their best to each other, and that the organisa tion should serve the client. One of the central facets in the process is providing employees with an overview of the financial status of the company. Although it is still in its early stages, there are indications that the process is making a substantial contribution to improving the climate of employee opinion.

Dup Moller, an engineer on site, commented on the process, known as 3H Indaba, in the following manner:

Part of the 3H Indaba is to get feedback from people about what is bothering them at the time. A few weeks after the Indaba we then hold a follow-up discussion with the people to give them feedback. At these feedback sessions it became clear that a number of the issues that were raised at the Indaba had been cleared up because people were now talking to each other. It is a fact that things have improved.

What I find most exciting about Safripol's success in turning around the climate of employee opinion, is the fact that they are located in an enormously conservative area and that they did this at a time of heightened political activity and tension.

Safripol has proved that this entire country still has a fighting chance at creating a future. We must stop thinking that our future will be delivered by politicians. We have to make that future or, more accurately, those in charge of the primary site of power, the workplace. The leadership at work are the people who have to make that future possible.

ABOUT THE AUTHOR

Etsko Schuitema is the founder of the Schuitema Group, a consultancy dedicated to the enhancement of human excellence based on the Care & Growth™ model.

Born into a mining family in South Africa, Etsko grew up in Johannesburg. After doing an Honours degree in Social Anthropology at the University of the Witwatersrand, he got a job as a graduate researcher with The Chamber of Mines of South Africa's Research Organisation.

Employed specifically by the Human Resources Laboratory of the organisation, his work initially focused on the issue of conflict on gold mines in South Africa. At the end of the overthrow of the apartheid regime, the mines were swept up in the upheaval that followed. The work he did led to the development of a framework for understanding trust in this very volatile environment.

Using this basis of this research he was asked to head the Human Resources Laboratory's Industry Project and implement his insights. This is where Care & Growth™ model originated. It was met with significant success within the mining sector. Such success in fact that Etsko left his role with the Chamber of Mines and along with a group of colleagues, to establish a consultancy where this model could be more widely disseminated.

Over the past 30 years, The Schuitema Group under the leadership of Etsko has, alongside several associates, worked in over 26 countries in a large range of sectors, creating powerful working relationships to implement the Care & Growth™ model empowering individuals on all levels of these organisations.

Etsko Schuitema is a renowned business consultant who has authored numerous books including 'Leadership' and 'The Millenium Discourses'. He is a senior partner in Schuitema, a transformational consultancy operating worldwide. Etsko is also a Shaykh or teacher in the Shadhili-Darqawi Sufi tradition and is known as Shaykh Ebrahim.

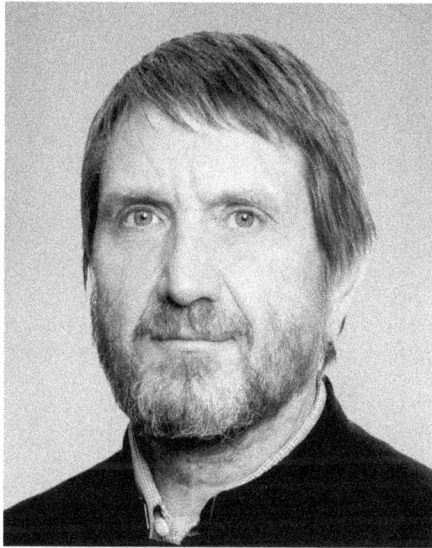

OTHER BOOKS BY ETSKO SCHUITEMA

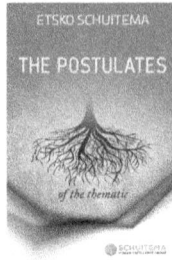

ETSKO SCHUITEMA

THE POSTULATES

of the thematic

SCHUITEMA

www.ingramcontent.com/pod-product-compliance
Lightning Source LLC
Chambersburg PA
CBHW022043190326
41520CB00008B/690